For Keeps

Women Tell the Truth
About Their Bodies, Growing Older, and Acceptance

edited by VICTORIA ZACKHEIM

SEAL PRESS

For Olivia and Sophia

May you always love and honor who you are.

For Keeps
Women Tell the Truth About Their Bodies, Growing Older, and Acceptance

Copyright © 2007 Victoria Zackheim

Published by Seal Press
A Member of Perseus Books Group
1400 65th Street, Suite 250
Emeryville, CA 94608

Library of Congress Cataloging-in-Publication Data

For keeps : women tell the truth about their bodies, growing older, and
acceptance / edited by Victoria Zackheim.
p. cm.
ISBN-13: 978-1-58005-204-7
ISBN-10: 1-58005-204-5
1. Middle-aged women—Psychology. 2. Middle-aged women—Attitudes. 3. Women—Psychology. 4.
Self-esteem in women. 5. Body image in women. I. Zackheim, Victoria.

HQ1059.4.F66 2007
306.4'613—dc22
2007032583

9 8 7 6 5 4 3 2 1

Cover design by Susan Koski Zucker
Interior design by Tabitha Lahr
Printed in the U.S.A.

Table of Contents

Introduction

Victoria Zackheim

A few months ago, I had my yearly mammogram. Breast cancer doesn't run in my family, so I usually await the "everything's fine" letter with little concern. When it arrived, I merely glanced at it, sure of its message, and then looked again and saw that I was to come back for another test.

A chilling sensation of dread ran through me. In the previous month, two dear friends had been diagnosed with breast cancer. Would I bring that number to three? Anxiety grew and I attempted to calm myself with the mantra *It's nothing It's nothing*, but if that were true, why was I eating everything in sight . . . and plenty stored behind cupboard doors? It was two weeks before they could fit me in for the follow-up mammogram, two long weeks before learning that I had dodged the bullet yet again. In that short, yet seemingly interminable, time, I learned this: To believe that I am healthy, to wish that I am healthy, and to live with the expectation that I will be healthy in no way guarantees my good health.

As much as we like to believe that we have full control of the circumstances of our lives—love, health, relationships—we do not. No matter how successful we are, how many books we have written or children we have launched, no matter how many business deals we've closed and illnesses or injuries we've overcome, life continues to remind us that the control we have fought so hard to attain can quickly slip away. And while many of us are able to regain that control, we cannot ignore the message that hovers out there, just beyond the coast of consciousness: Our bodies are for keeps. No matter what life brings us, we must forge ahead and celebrate life.

Before you begin to read this anthology and share the journey of more than two dozen gifted writers, I ask you to consider this: With everything the world throws at us, imagine how wonderful it would be if we women could stop struggling with negative feelings about ourselves. This book takes a big step in that direction. Every one of these authors has reminded us that we *can* be positive, we *can* face illness, injury, and the sometimes insidious signs of aging, and feel wonderful about ourselves.

And therein lies the heart of this book.

For Keeps emerged from my belief that our bodies and souls are woven into one beautiful and often bewildering pattern, and that life for many women would be less stressful and more fulfilling if we knew how to live in our bodies, accept our bodies, and stop viewing ourselves through an out-of-focus lens. It was my wish to create a book in which women of all ages could write about courage and dignity, about overcoming physical and emotional hardship, including injury and illness, depression and age, and share with you their insights hard-won through that battle we call *life*.

Too many of us go through life worrying more about taut stomachs than about healthy aging; we fret more about society's expectations than our own personal growth. Perhaps this is because, whether we're young girls or elderly women, we are bombarded by the media's idea of perfection: lithe young models with perfect skin and smooth bodies too often achieved through eating disorders and fad diets, or older women maintaining that illusion through plastic surgery and Botox treatments. No matter what product a manufacturer is trying to sell, the substance of that message remains the same: Women are imperfect, and, unless we succumb to the hype, that imperfection will thwart our chances for happiness.

We see and hear this message as we move from girl to woman, the loping and freely moving gait of childhood shifting into something choreographed and self-conscious. We are always aware of it, and our walk becomes more studied. We want to flow with grace as we emulate an older sister, an admired babysitter, a model, our mother, or some actress. If we pursue athletics or dance, we are proud when our bodies reflect this. But what happens when our bodies let us down and we find ourselves—our spirit and sometimes our will to live—tested? Do we crumble under the weight of the bad news, or do we become stronger, more determined? Whether our obstacle is physical injury or illness, emotional turmoil or negative attitudes about our bodies, the result can be the same: misery and insecurity.

Liza Nelson had always struggled with having large breasts. In *Divorcing My Breasts* she writes, "Who would I have been at thirty with trim breasts and a body that didn't shame me? Would I have been less socially awkward, less afraid to take career risks, less tense?" When she was faced with a possible double mastectomy, her response shocked many friends who thought they knew her so well. Liza was about to embark on a journey that taught her unexpected lessons about herself.

Our society views a bout of pneumonia with more compassion than it does a battle against depression, and yet Americans suffer depression and mental illness in large numbers. For many families, it exists as a dark secret never to be revealed. For those who struggle toward the light, where do they find the strength and the courage? In *Surviving the Spiral*, Regina Anavy writes, "Morning arrives and you do not feel rested. Time becomes meaningless, for you are wrapped in the time zone of depression, your own private misery. The simplest act becomes a struggle: getting out of bed; brushing your teeth; combing your hair; dressing. Sheer maintenance wears you out. You are alone, falling faster into inner space." In the telling of her story, she reminds us that there is a way to recover our emotional footing.

So many of us experience moments, years, even a lifetime of poor body image. Most of us know women—friend, sister, neighbor, ourselves—whose health has been damaged by the powerful need to be in control of their lives. Sometimes the effects are obvious, such as the wasting away caused by bulimia or anorexia. Other times, the results can be less visible. For Aimee Liu, tall and beautiful and destroying her body through unrelenting exercise and near-starvation, the outcome was nearly catastrophic. In *Dead Bone* she reveals, "The more my body hurt, the more my willpower gloated. A war was underway, my physical constitution its battleground. Health was no more my real goal than cheap tea was the object of the American Revolution."

We women are so hard on ourselves. We take those damning messages about the ideal woman and apply them to our lives and our bodies. In *What I Gave Up*, Ellen Sussman reveals how she tormented herself because she wasn't perfect. "Instead of Zen thinking, I sat in yoga class, day after day, week after week, thinking murderous thoughts: *Why can't I do this? Why can everyone else?*"

There are times when our control is so dramatically snatched away that we wonder if we shall ever regain it. Louisa Ermelino addresses this loss with dignity and humor in *Death Becomes Her*. "My mother is dying in her bed across the street. . . . My husband is in the hospital, defying the medical prediction that he had six months to live. It's been ten and we're still counting. Me, I'm going back and forth from the hospital to my mother's bedside to my job at a celebrity fashion magazine. Is Nicole Kidman wearing Zac Posen, and did she really buy her lasagna pan at Williams-Sonoma?" When you read her story, you will discover how one woman found the courage and the humor to keep going.

Many of the women in this book have experienced complicated and sometimes grating relationships with their mothers. Several of the authors have looked back on the mother-daughter relationship as the source of their poor self-image. In Carrie Kabak's *Every Eyelash, Mole, and Freckle*, she writes about her mother with devastating clarity. "She pinches a piece of the fabric, her mouth forming an upside down U in disgust, then she wipes her hands down each side of her skirt, like she's just touched dirt. Confused, I look down at my body. But the dress skims the new curves I have now. The seams swerve to a tiny waist and spread with a gentle flare over my hips. This yellow cardigan goes so well with it—I thought she loved this combination, she definitely said so last week . . ."

The women who have written about living through the spectrum of physical, emotional, and spiritual challenges have done so with honesty, courage, and generosity. They remind us that a woman's inner strength is a driving force in a world that expects too little of us. Read on and you will meet twenty-seven women who wrote their hearts out while addressing this very subject, women who share with us the gift of their profound, sometimes hilarious, and always engaging stories. Perhaps even more important, each woman has tapped into a tender and meaningful place within her, revealing how she faced her own personal adversity and moved on. Through these stories, you will find yourself nodding, laughing, sometimes gasping in disbelief as you read intimate reflections on how body image, illness, injury, and depression have changed, and in many ways enriched, their lives.

It is my sincere wish that you read these pages with an open heart. Some of us have stumbled—this is, after all, real life!—and all of us have shared some transformative event that reminds us of the importance of accepting our body and living joyful and productive lives.

Every Eyelash, Mole, and Freckle
Carrie Kabak

There is one taboo that has withstood all the recent efforts at demystification:
the idealization of mother love.
—Alice Miller

My mother's eyes follow the lines of my dress, and I can tell my body passes inspection this time, because my hair receives more attention now.

"Trudy was surprised when she met you last week," she says. "You were not what she expected."

Trudy, Trudy, Trudy. These days I have to eat, sleep, and drink Trudy. Now that I have finally met her, she's even part of my dreams. She towers above me in distorted perspective, her legs thinner than bamboo and I a splodge at her feet.

So. Trudy was surprised. Looking on the bright side, this could mean she was amazed. But no. Trudy pictured me with urchin features, apparently. A little pointed face under a mop of black curls. All my mother's fault, who, before the fatal encounter, probably waxed lyrical over my appearance and achievements in life—to boost her own ego, mainly. Unfortunately, my looks didn't measure up, and now Mum is disappointed. Even embarrassed.

"Trudy thought you would look more like me," she says, fluffing her thick, slate-gray hair. She stands sideways and sucks in her stomach. "You haven't said a word about the amount of weight I've lost."

"Wow, Mum, I do see a huge difference. You look fantastic."

I am the source for much-needed admiration and adulation. She's insatiable.

Mum may marvel at my thin ankles, but her hips are neater. My eyes may be larger, but her hands are finer. Her hair is dense, but mine? "It's so lifeless, darling." She lifts a strand of it now, lets it fall, and I flinch.

"But you said the blond streaks did a lot for me!" *Make your mind up, Mum.*

"Not with that dress. What made you wear that thing *again*, when you knew you might bump into Trudy?" She pinches a piece of the fabric, her mouth forming an upside-down U in disgust, and then she wipes her hands down each side of her skirt, like she's just touched dirt. Confused, I look down at my body. But the dress skims the new curves I have. The seams swerve to a tiny waist and spread with a gentle flare over my hips. This yellow cardigan goes so well with it—I thought she loved this combination; she definitely said so last week. . . .

"The color is too close to your hair dye," she says. "Makes you look washed out. No wonder Trudy wasn't impressed."

Fuck Trudy.

Today, I brought only one dress with me. I usually throw two in the car, or a pair of pants, just in case Mum says the first choice makes my hips look twice as wide, or it rides up my backside, or the shoulder pads make me look like Mr. Universe. *If you think that suits you, then you're wrong.*

It's different when I'm away from her, in the privacy of my own home, with my friends and family, on my own ground. When I'm comfortable in my own skin, happily indifferent about slopping around the house in old jeans or an oversize T-shirt and nothing much else. Bare feet. Oh, of course I'm at war with my body at times—who isn't? Wanting to be half my size to slip into a slinky gown, or peel on supertight pants and still look good. But I'm disgruntled and fed up, not distraught. I rarely obsess or hate myself.

I only do that when I'm with Mum. Yes, I'm crazy. I'll admit to being a gibbering, appeasing twit. The day before I'm to meet up with her, something comes over me. As Skeeter Davis might say:

> *She asks if I love her*
> *I don't know how to say*
> *Just how much I love her,*
> *so let me prove it this way.*

I panic, frantically book a last-minute haircut, slap on a face mask. Scrub away at dry skin, manicure, shave legs—have

I forgotten anything? I *want* to be that image in her head. That perfect daughter.

And all I can think now, as I stand in the driveway, is, *Sod it!* My hair is straw, my dress is a limp rag, my face is a white mess. With shoulders hunched, I walk with my mother toward the house. You see, it ruins my visits when I don't look good—when Mum doesn't approve. Why can't I get it right? *Especially* today.

"Stand up straight," she says. "*Yoo-hoo, Trudy!*"

Trudy, stick-thin Trudy, flutters a delicate hand from a bony wrist. Let me fill you in: She's the new neighbor, same age as me, in her mid-forties—no, I'm not a child—and she is the latest surrogate daughter. The replacement for when I let my mother down, the substitute for when my mother hasn't seen my face for fifteen days, let alone received one phone call. The option who didn't have children who demanded constant attention, or who too often had a baby drinking at her breast. The standby who didn't give birth to four children, one after the other, making it sound like she lived on a back street.

My children. I leaped into motherhood, filled my arms and heart with children, reveling in their unconditional love. My one stand. Or rebellion, or even defiance.

"My poor daughter," Mum would say, "with her face and abdomen so swollen. Unfortunately, she has toxemia, Mrs. Digby-Phillips."

No, I wasn't riddled with bacterial toxins at the time; I was roundly eight months pregnant and my mother was ashamed of me—too obvious and so much bigger than she when she carried me. Mum wore neat little overblouses at the time, and no one guessed she was expecting. Am I wearing a good supportive bra under that tent? I look so puffed and podgy.

She never had zits. I did. Her feet are small, as light as a pixie's. Mine are flat and wide. She elevates herself to appear superior in comparison. I don't mirror her in looks or choice of lifestyle, which saddens her.

Yes, she's a handful. Incorrigible, irredeemable, but I keep coming back for more, feeding her need, desperately wanting her to love me.

*   *   *

And now.

Now, the tingle of a breeze brings me back to my parents' garden. Spots of rain fall, and a watery sun drops rivers of light into every corner, highlighting the pruned twigs, the mulched shrubs, and the pieced patchwork of heather. All under control. Managed, scrutinized, forced, and supervised. Mum has managed to make the garden beautiful, but I swear, she feels she has failed miserably with me. I listen as she shouts over the hedge. Her special voice undulates, her posh version for Trudy, who shoots deer and hunts foxes on horseback and has a swimming pool. Mum must give the impression that she, too, is oh-so-charming, intelligent, and incredibly well connected. "Off to aerobics?" she says, her face aghast. "Oh, Trudy, now what do *you* have to worry about?"

Looking awfully like a praying mantis in that leotard, maybe.

Mum, skilled at presenting the respectable, sweet public face, can even be meek and mild if it's called for. It's often hard to believe she can scream like a demented banshee behind closed doors.

I check my watch and swallow hard. I will have to face her fury in about an hour. Maybe less. *Boom, boom, boom* goes my head, before it settles down to an incessant throb. I always get headaches before thunderstorms. I press my thumbs to my temples to ease the pain, to help me think and take stock—and reality hits me in the pit of my stomach with a sickening blow. *This could be the last time I ever see Mum, depending on how things go.* Damn the way this dress makes me look. Or would my appearance have made any difference? I tell myself not to be so bloody stupid. I try to dilute my feelings of dread. How much longer . . . ?

I peer over the hedge to see Trudy's hand resting on the handle of her car door. Can't she just go, for God's sake? Slipping into the background, I find a good hiding place under a plum tree, not wishing to confabulate with the latest golden child.

Trudy, poor dear, is the third surrogate, I think. They last only so long. They come and go but are usually incredibly cute, or have beautiful limbs, and are always full of life and personality, treating Mum and Dad like *real* parents. When I roll my eyes, the trouble with me, my girl, is that I'm green with jealousy. "She *is,* Bill," Mum will say to my father, who is humble to the extreme.

There's the roar of an engine at last. Trudy's on her way. Thank you, God.

"Where are you?" calls Mum.

"I'm here." I circle a flower bed to reach her.

"Nice shoes," she says, smiling, showing dimples and the gap between her front teeth. She takes my face in her hands and plants rapid kisses on my forehead, and then she holds me, rocks me. I crave every second of my mother's sporadic approval. Her method of affection is best described as a controlling passion. This sixty-eight-year-old woman hurts, insults, brings tears to my eyes, but I'm always in overwhelming need of her love, no matter how stifling. The sweet always follows the sour. Smiles follow sneers, gentleness follows gibes—you know I love you, she says. Spontaneous hugs follow spite. Arms will squeeze and then tug like a reprimand, insisting I squeeze back. It's pathetic, really. I am totally in awe of this woman. In love with her. Dependent on her. She made me like this.

But this display is good. This moment. My confidence increases by a hair's breadth—*God, how I want to get this over and done with. I'll just come straight out with it, that's best. During dinner.*

Mum inspects my chin through her bifocals. "The electrolysis is leaving pockmarks. Why do you bother?"

I shrug, deciding to keep the real reason to myself. Electrolysis is yet another of my attempts to gain approval. "You said you saw a few black hairs five months ago," I say. She was right: There were four.

You see, Mum, I want skin like yours, you who have never put a smear of makeup on your face, let alone a bottle of dye to your hair, because you have never needed such things. Unlike me.

The rain has become fine and constant. "We'd better go in," she says. "The casserole should be ready by now."

I don't recall this unique kind of attention when I was a child—it all started when I reached puberty, I think. They *can't* be period pains. Not possible. How does she know? She has my dates marked on a calendar. Why? So she knows when to pick up a packet of tampons from the pharmacy, that's all. And she would kiss my cheek.

This woman knows the very timetable of my body. She's familiar with every root of hair on my head, every toenail, every eyelash, every mole and freckle. The invasion is both comfortable—this is her method of loving me, isn't it?—and disconcerting at the same time.

This may be the last time I see her.

The house is toasty when we step inside. Mum doesn't want my help, so I wander off to the living room. The fireplace yawns widely, exposing a grate, like teeth, where flames crackle and sparks tumble. Outside, the rain is much heavier now, falling in slanted sheets.

My husband is at a crickethockeygolfsquash match, I can't remember which, today. Although that will be canceled now, I'm thinking.

Ha! Speaking of which, never mind the management, Mum even influenced my decision regarding who should *use* my body—the only one of myriad boyfriends she favored. Back then, anyway. She hates my husband now.

My eldest children—two of my reasons for staying in the marriage so long—have new cars, so they disappeared this morning, too. The other two reasons are with friends playing video games—I needed to be alone with my mother today. Didn't want them witnessing a terrible scene. And it will be sensational.

There's a roll. A spike of lightning. The thunderstorm has started. The knot at the back of my neck unravels. My head will feel better soon. *Good job.* I need all my wits about me. I shall soon make the decision of a lifetime.

Not long now. I can smell the casserole. Despite being a lapsed Catholic—correction, a heathen (yes, you've guessed it, "heathen" is my mother's description of me)—I still pray. With whom—or Whom with a capital W—I'm actually talking, I never know, but please let there be some benevolent, supreme being listening in now. *Please, God, help me with this.*

*   *   *

I took a huge step, more than half a year ago, by moving to the attic, away from the "marital bed," as my husband calls it. He wasn't too bothered, which raises vague suspicion, but that doesn't matter now. Mum knows about the separation, for want of a better word. She's delighted, in fact, because, as she joked last week, she has her daughter back now. "Yikes" was the word that jumped to my mind. She had it all planned. Why don't I move to the same street as my parents? There's a house coming up for sale only three doors down! *Aw, shit, I don't think so.* A bedroom each for the children, she said. A nice garden. Now, I love my mother with a vengeance, I do, but I couldn't live *that* close.

I have to space my visits, or I'd go mad. But that isn't what I've come to tell her today. It's something else. And what I am about to tell her will send her over the edge.

"Dinner's ready," she calls.

"Looks wonderful, Mum." Rich gravy, pearl onions, mashed potatoes, bubbling hot. She *is* the best cook. I sink into a chair. Right. Now is as good a time as any, while we're occupied, eating. I promised myself I'd blurt it straight out. Here goes.

"I met a man. He's forty-seven. He is divorced, he has a teenage son, and I love him."

I fish in my handbag and put a photo on the table, by the side of her plate.

There.

"We're going to get married."

As soon as we can. But enough information for now.

It will take her some time to absorb this. "Start eating before it gets cold," she says.

Oh.

The rain beats hard at the windows. She studies the image of the man who adores every square inch of me. I don't have to earn points for *his* love. My soul mate. My lover.

We eat. A few words are exchanged about the sudden storm. This is sheer hell—what is going on here? We chew and drink in silence until the last piece of carrot is finished. "Well, this is a nice surprise," she says finally, her face solid stone. "It's too soon. You're not even divorced yet. Have you slept with this man?"

I look at her steadily. I don't have to answer this. *Be strong.*

"Well?" she says.

I have to be careful. She's waiting for my answer and will listen with studied intensity to my very breath, voice intonation, and choice of words. If she detects guilt, then she has me. For once, and God, I deserve this, I want *some* privacy. I will not answer the question. *Aw, hell, no good;* her face is creased with distaste. She's already taken it for granted.

"Slut," she says under her breath.

We have discussed sex, when she takes the opportunity to express her reserve and coyness with my father. We've talked about the disinterest I experienced with my husband. And we can ridicule sex, but we mustn't like it. But now here I sit, no longer the Virgin Mary like her, no longer the same—barely unsullied, rarely touched. I wait for the next insult from she who covers her crotch with one hand if I catch her unawares in an unlocked bathroom. She who has never stripped *completely* naked in front of my father, apparently.

I learned to hide my body, too—not to the same extent, but I was never proud of it. Never flaunted it. Until recently.

Mum takes another look at the photo. I brace myself.

"You're hopeless at choosing men, aren't you? Never been any good at it." She proceeds to criticize my man's stature and features, using cruel, brutal words, with primitive wrath and hostility. Rage follows. Threats, ultimatums, and when that's not enough, for I haven't weakened and started crying yet, she snarls, and when I try to interject, she imitates my voice.

This may be the last time I see her, I remind myself. And you know? I'm ready for it.

"I'm *forty-six!*" I finally manage to yell. "It's my body, Mum, and I'm old enough to do the hell what I like with it!"

My body now. Not hers, not my soon-to-be-ex's, but mine. My poor body. It swelled with gestation, it stretched, it ripped, it was cut and sewn up, prodded at, observed. After the last child, a hysterectomy. Used by an indifferent spouse occasionally. Then the appendectomy. I'm amazed it ever recovered.

Mum bangs the table with her fist, sends a fork skidding to the floor. It's. Too. Soon. Do I hear her? She will strike me from her will if I go any further with this man; what do I think of that, eh? She will cut me out of her life. Forever. What's more, should I die before her, she wouldn't even bother to visit my grave to spit on it.

The thunder is an explosion overhead, a deafening crack. Now I bawl like an idiot. Mum? Dear God. *Mum?* I howl like an abandoned child. I sob, cry out, until my neck throbs, my stomach hurts, until I'm reduced to shaking silently with my face in my hands.

After what seems like hours but surely is mere minutes, with wavering sighs I actually manage to pull myself together. I clench my fists, jut out my chin, feeling mysteriously cleansed. It's over. I did it, and it went wrong, but *hell,* I tell myself, *I damn well knew it would.* It's time to make the decision of a lifetime. Time to accept. Time to change. A cloud lifts, a big, black, heavy one, and when I look at my mother's seething face, pale with anger, I give her a quiet goodbye. She taps her fingernails on the table, her critical eye checking my walk, my posture, as I fetch my keys. I sense she has no idea of the strength or significance that goodbye holds. She will confidently believe I'll be back, sorry tail wagging.

I walk out the back door.

Even more clouds have ganged up to darken the sky, dropping sharper needles of rain now. When I reach my car, I sob again. I sob my heart out, because my mother can't see the tears now, can she? And that's the important thing. She will never see me cry again.

This was the day I cut all ties and left her for good.

For a while, I mourned the loss of what could have been, or what normally—yes, *normally*—should have been. I fell out of love with her after coming to the painful realization that I was nothing more than an instrument of self-gratification, as easily discarded as a cigarette end.

But my body and mental health are so much better for it.

I am at peace.

Impossible Geometry
Margot Beth Duxler

im·pos·si·ble: not capable of happening or being done.
ge·om·e·try: the mathematics of the properties, measurement, and
  relationships of points, lines, angles, surfaces, and solids.

Impossible Geometry depicts constructions and relationships
between objects that defy reality. Though more related
to mathematics and art, examples of Impossible Geometry
are numerous in beginning psychology textbooks. One is a
three-dimensional drawing of a fork in which one of the tines
appears to be simultaneously behind and in front of the others.
It is the impossibility of these parallel realities that challenges
and may alter our definitions of what is real and of ourselves.
Artist M. C. Escher popularized these impossible constructions
in many of his drawings, in which stairs climb and descend at
the same time, archways advance while receding, and birds fly
in multiple directions simultaneously.

* * *

What makes these images so intriguing is their depiction of a reality that just cannot be. And the very qualities that make our perceptions want to reject them also make them compelling. The mind wants to make sense of them. To see and to understand. Create a file we can access at will.

Impossible Geometry is the stuff of which horror films are made. Love stories, too. Some things are just not supposed to happen. But they can, and they do.

April 1, 2004

"How are you feeling?" the anesthesiologist asks. Her fingers are deft. No pain as she inserts the needle. "You'll begin to feel the drug almost immediately."

It's April Fools' Day. I chose it. I love the irony. Be careful. Swift current. Granite-cold liquid courses through my veins. A tributary of the Yuba River at the beginning of snowmelt. Her eyes are beautiful above her mask. Green with flecks of gold. Like the river in midsummer. I try to answer her question, though I know she is asking pro forma to help me relax. She can't be more than fourteen years old. Her skin is unwrinkled, white and peach. "Butterflies," I say, knowing I make no sense to her. "Butterflies." I'm floating now, on my big yellow-and-violet raft in the deep pool at the Bridgeport crossing.

"Butterflies?" She is gauging my state of somnolence. Or perhaps my sanity.

*   *   *

"You're great," I answer, wading into her eyes. I let go of
the raft. She will have to keep me afloat.

Pt. Name: Duxler, Margot Beth
DOB: 6/28/1948
Sex: F
Visit: #2
Operation Date: 4/1/04
Clinical Indications: This fifty-five-year-old woman presents with
palpitations. Echocardiogram shows a large left atrial myxoma.

Heart of gold. Bleeding heart. Purple heart. Heart of
stone. Fearless heart. Broken heart. The heart of the matter. In
a heartbeat. Images of love at the body's core. The residence
of the soul.

March 3, 2004

I am chatting with Cindy, the echocardiogram technician.
She's a dog person. I'm a cat person. In the extreme. We
trade stories of animals lost and found. Of early-warning
earthquake alarms manifested in spirals of barking at changes
in sound, smell, light waves. A cat, deep in sleep, launching
off the sofa like a slice of bread rocketing out of an overly
springy toaster slot. We talk about loss. My Albert, buried
now in our garden in Grass Valley beneath a headless old
church statue of St. Francis of Assisi. Albert died in my arms,
with my husband Michael's arms around me. We wanted to be

with him when he crossed over. He'd been suffering too long with a slow and pernicious form of congestive heart failure. Dr. Kitty Kevorkian, in the person of Dr. Julio Bolivar-Dillon, set Albert's soul free from his infirm, suffering body. Our liberating angel. Cindy understands. I know she's thinking about her dogs, Fred and Jake.

As she sets up the equipment, I explain that I've been having palpitations. I assume they were caused by hormones. What isn't at my age? But one day they persist. Through a full day of psychotherapy patients—unrequited love, the boss from hell, an abusive mother, kleptomania, depression—*thump-thump. Thump-thump-thump. Thumpthumpthumpthump.*

"I felt like I had a flock of butterflies beating against my rib cage, desperately trying to free themselves," I say, wondering absently if butterflies flock.

"What an image," she says. "You know those butterfly trees in Pacific Grove?" she asks.

During migration they are covered with saffron and onyx monarchs. Thousands of them. Beautiful. From a distance. To me, they're still insects. But I just smile.

Cindy begins the baseline test. She is quiet now. Concentrating.

* * *

I grew up in Chicago. Minutes or even hours before a thunderstorm, you can feel it in the air. The atmosphere smells blue, and your exposed arms and legs vibrate slightly with a mercurial electricity. Something about Cindy's breathing changes. I can smell the ozone in the air. It is anxiety. Hers. I feel suddenly cold, my arms all goosefleshy. The hair on the back of my neck stands up as it would before an impending lightning strike. If I were a cat, I'd spring straight up off this table.

Cindy puts a hand on my shoulder. *Oh, shit.* "I'll be right back," she says. "I'm going to ask Dr. Kersh to come in." Her voice is tight as a saw blade. I am grateful for her touch. She can't look at me as she leaves the room.

When the door closes, I stretch around to see the monitor. Whatever it is I'm looking at is incomprehensible to me. It's not a Rorschach. Not a projective test. Something on that screen is objectively bad. I don't know how to make sense of the black-and-white shadows. The door opens and Cindy comes back in with Dr. Kersh. She points to the screen.

"Hmm," he says. "Uh huh."

Those are my lines, I think, a feeble attempt to amuse myself. Fortunately, I have enough control to not say it out loud.

"Get dressed and meet me in my office," Dr. Kersh says softly. He leaves the room.

*   *   *

I know better than to ask Cindy to reveal the mystery on the screen. Her kindness in helping me off the examining table makes me want to cry. We are no longer peers. Our accord is unspoken and clear. My passport has been stamped. In an instant I have emigrated from the land of the healthy to the land of the ill.

"Please, just say it," I tell Dr. Kersh, before I'm even seated in the chair across the desk from him.

"A myxoma," he says.

I trained at a hospital-based psychiatric clinic. I know enough medicine to understand "myxoma" much too clearly. "A tumor," I say, absurdly aware of wanting to impress him.

He nods his head. "The good news is that these tumors are almost always benign."

Almost always. Almost. It rattles around like a penny in a tin box.

"Then I guess there's nothing to worry about," I say. *Rattle, rattle.*

"The bad news is that it has to come out."

His words are a kick in the stomach from a mule with new shoes. I hear wind under leathery wings, anticipate the tearing beak and claws. Pterodactyl time! Run for cover! I begin to babble. "Oh. So is this a laparoscopic procedure? Quick in-and-out? Or is it treated chemically?" I know that I'm stalling. I may as well throw in my mother's recipe for lemon meringue pie and the "Charge of the Light Brigade" I had to memorize in fourth grade.

"No. It's open-heart surgery. Bypass. The works."

My car mechanic has a better bedside manner than this poor man, delivering his horror-movie news. "I have a tumor on my heart," I mumble. I'm trying not to cry. This cannot be possible.

"No, actually," he says gently now, needing me to understand and wanting to prevent a meltdown in his consulting room, "it's *in* your heart."

April 1, 2004
PROCEDURE COMPLETED

Procedure: The patient was brought to the operating room and placed in a comfortable supine position on the operating table, and general anesthesia induced without difficulty.

March 3, 2004

I feel unreal as I leave the echo lab. The world is flat and I'm afraid I might fall off the edge. I make a mental list: *Arrange coverage for my patients. What will I tell them? How much? What if I don't come back? Some will ask. What if I don't come back? Heidi's birthday is tomorrow, my all-grown-up foster daughter. Have to wait awhile to tell her. My brother. Our parents died when he was so young, Father when he was only eighteen, Mother when he was twenty-five. He has a good marriage, twin girls. He's okay.*

Michael. *Hi, Love. I changed my mind about Paris. I'd rather have open-heart surgery.* We found each other late in life. We learned to waltz. On Shabbos we play music together, he guitar, I violin. We fight, rarely. "I'm sorry if you're sorry." And we're dancing again.

*   *   *

Suddenly, I understand something I've always accepted as fact but that I now know is wrong. About animals "going off to die." *He knew he was dying and he ran away.* When Albert was sick, and then sicker, we would find him at the back of the linen closet. Squeezed beneath the armoire, where there was barely enough room for a deck of cards. Nearly flattened between the washing machine and the dryer. Now I understand. Animals don't know that they're dying. They can't distinguish pain that is inflicted by an external predator and pain that is visited from within. They run to get away from the pain. They are trying to save their lives.

March 4, 2004
ARE KARMA KICKBACK CHICKENS THE ONES WHO COME HOME TO ROOST?

The river runs flecked with gold; the current is lively, playful. I don't anticipate the rapids around the next bend. I mistake falling leaves for hummingbirds. The river changes course without warning. I'm a cliché, yet when I hit the falls, I don't ever think of asking, *Why me? What have I done to deserve this? What kind of bad behavior is this payback for?* Before I call Michael to tell him about the tumor, and even later on, I don't for one second think about these questions. I do, however, obsess intermittently about why nothing horrible has ever happened to my evil cousin Jacquie. She's who Oscar Wilde had in mind for *The Picture of Dorian Gray.* Only Jacquie didn't sell her soul to the devil, because she never had one to begin with. Jacquie actually thinks that illness of any kind is a character flaw. I can hardly believe that I want something terrible and painful (and really ugly would be a great bonus!) to happen to her, but I do.

March 5, 2004
SCRAMBLED, FRIED, OR OVER EASY?

Michael does all the research to find the right surgeon. He can't tolerate helplessness. He's thorough and fast, let loose on the Internet, calling colleagues and friends. He finds Dr. Scot Merrick at the University of California, San Francisco Medical Center. I'm relieved that the best is close to home.

I remember absolutely nothing about my preoperative consultation, other than Dr. Merrick's calm, slightly Southern voice, his musician's fingers, and the bathroom down the hall where I spend most of the meeting vomiting while Michael asks all the questions. I was reasonably all right until Dr. Merrick says, "The tumor appears to be about the size of an egg." An egg? A chicken egg? Karma kickback chickens. *Send them to Jacquie,* I think, wishing terrible things on her again. If anyone deserves to be karmalized, it is she! An egg can't possibly fit in my heart! My body has betrayed me. I shoot out of my chair. "Bathroom" is all I say. From unreal to too real. My stomach is empty but I can't stop gagging, afraid that if I leave the bathroom my body will humiliate me, as if betrayal is not enough. When I return to Dr. Merrick's office and sit down next to Michael, I hum "I Left My Heart in San Francisco," just loud enough for him to hear. He smiles, just barely.

Heartthrob. Heartsick. Heartache. Heartless. Hearty. Heartfelt.

There are giant valentine-shaped hearts on display all over the city: Hearts in San Francisco, a fund-raiser for San Francisco General Hospital. I like the timing. They help me feel hopeful. Big, fat, colorful hearts. Openness. Tolerance. Love. Hearts are everywhere. At a bead fair at Fort Mason, I buy dozens of varicolored glass hearts, none larger than my thumbnail: red, turquoise, shimmery gold, silver, violet, Venetian glass with tiny flowers embedded in the center. I glue them into the recesses of an old shadow box, making sure the glue holds fast so none of them falls out. Homage to the inevitable, whatever it turns out to be.

March 28, 2004
A WALK IN THE PARK

The Sunday before surgery. Michael and I take a walk in Golden Gate Park. We touch each other constantly, memorizing our aliveness. A young couple is a few yards ahead of us. Two lovely girls, arguing about something. I can't hear what they're saying. Their body language is angry, reactive. They stop walking to yell at each other on the side of the path. *Don't fight.* I want to tell them to hold each other and make up, but I pretend I don't notice them as Michael and I walk past.

March 31, 2004
THE GIFTS OF THE MAGI ARE NOT AUCTIONED ON EBAY

If hope is that thing with feathers (thanks, Emily), love is that thing with broad shoulders, a strong back, and a sense of humor. In the O. Henry story "The Gift of the Magi," Della cuts off and sells her magnificent hair to buy her husband, Jim, a watch fob for Christmas. Unaware of his wife's sacrifice, Jim pawns his watch to buy Della a set of tortoiseshell combs to set off her crowning glory. Oops.

The day before surgery. I'm cleaning the cat litter. We have two cats: Matilda, whom Albert left behind when he died, and Benny, our newly adopted kitten. The cats have been very busy. I decide that I want to spend today quietly, just resting, napping with the cats, maybe writing, playing a little music with Michael.

Michael has gone out to buy a pager. A pager! He has two business phone numbers, a fax number, and a cell phone that he carries on his person at all times, as if it were the remote control. This is 2004! What the fuck does he need a pager for?

And all at once I understand the formula. I'm standing at the top of the stairs with a bag full of cat shit, and I get it. More gadgets equal more control. He's scared to death he's going to lose me. He's more terrified than I am.

Now I'm panicky. I call all his numbers. He doesn't pick up. Tomorrow morning the surgical team will stop my heart. Shit! What if there's an earthquake? I begin to sob. And I realize that I haven't cried since the diagnosis. Where the hell is he?

*   *   *

And then the door bursts open. I've been complaining to him for years to open the door quietly: *You stomp up the stairs like a tyrannosaurus!* He bounds up the steps with noisy, great big feet. We wrap around each other, weave into each other's arms. I still have the bag of cat shit in my hand. The romance of long-term love.

"No one even sells pagers anymore," he whispers. "I thought you wanted to be alone." He's crying softly.

"I thought you needed to get away." I'm crying too.

"You moron," he says.

"You're the moron!" I say.

Then, simultaneously, "I'm one if you're one!"

April 1, 2004
PROCEDURE COMPLETED

After verifying sponge and needle count . . . sterile dressings were applied and the patient taken to the intensive care unit in satisfactory condition.

September 11, 2006
EMOTIONAL GEOMETRY

Today is Monday, September 11, the fifth anniversary of Global Impossible Geometry. Friends call from New York, Paris, Chicago. We remember together the apocalyptic, and ask about children, spouses, lovers, pets. The geographical distances don't matter. The geometry of our points, lines, angles, surfaces, and solids is resilient and reliable.

Last Friday, September 8: My third postoperative echocardiogram. Cindy is my good-luck charm. She shows me the monitor. "There," she points. "If I didn't know for a fact you'd had heart surgery, I'd never believe it. There's not even any scar tissue!"

Thank you, Dr. Merrick.

She tells me that Fred is moving slower these days. She can see it, but her husband insists he's just fine. I admire her screen-saver pictures of Jake and Fred and promise to bring pictures of the cats to my appointment next year.

*   *   *

My scar is silver and runs six inches down the middle of my chest. My Excalibur. My bolt of lightning. My Cupid's arrow. Today, especially, I am aware of luck and the variables of geometry that enabled me to pass through the arches, up and down the stairs, to observe the birds migrating in multiple directions simultaneously.

Ex-Large

Christine Kehl O'Hagan

For most of her life, my mother was thin—although her thinness was hard won. She was the only one of four children to survive, and her Irish mother was not about to lose her, too, and so my grandmother weighed my mother down with too much food and wrapped her carefully in fat. Mom's extended family often teased her—"slipped the mickey," as the Irish put it. One would think that a little girl who had lost three brothers might be spared the mickey, but our Irish family offered few exemptions. They called her "Platter Puss." The Irish tongue cuts like no other, and when my mother was sixteen, she put herself on a milk-and-soup diet and lost fifty pounds. For the rest of her life, Mom claimed to weigh not 120 pounds, but 119, and said she was a "perfect size 10"—even when she was nearly eighty and could hardly zip the back of a size 18.

Although Mom "ran a fine table" for everyone else, she ate very little herself and, more often than not, snuffed out her cigarette in the remains of a dinner that was tiny to begin with.

Fat people made Mom shudder—especially Aunt Nellie, who lived in the apartment house next door and was too old for "the mickey" and too fat to wear anything but the same old brown dress. Then there was Cousin Howard, who was not only fat, but clumsy. One ancient New Year's Eve, Cousin Howard sat on the highball he'd left on his chair, which guaranteed him years of mickey slipping, since everyone knew that Howard, who'd had urogenital surgery years earlier, was down one to begin with.

One might think, therefore, that a mother who had struggled so with weight would do whatever it took to help her daughter stay slim, and she might have—if I hadn't nearly died, at age four, of a ruptured appendix. No sooner had I left the hospital than my mother and my grandmother began "building me up" with the all-purpose Irish cure of dairy products, cod liver oil, White's Multi-Vi drops, and red, bloody meat.

When I was ten, I was as tall as my mother and could no longer fit in her shoes. When the other girls were clomping around in their mothers' high heels, my mother, had she wanted to, could have clomped around in my Catholic school oxfords.

The year I was twelve, I was as tall as my father, a blue-collar dandy who wore bow ties on weekends and, depending on the season, wore either wool or seersucker suits to Sunday Mass. That year, to my younger sister and younger brother's great amusement, I was able to pick my father up and move him somewhere else whenever he blocked the doorway of our small kitchen.

Though my parents were happy that I was healthy and strong, having a broad daughter who was just under six feet tall was not in their plan, and they didn't know quite what to do with me.

My mother blamed my size on my Yankee father's side, for my Dutch-reformed father came from what my Roman Catholic grandmother called "black-hearted Protestants," referring mainly to Dad's Uncle Tom (a.k.a. "Blackie") Kehl, one of the tallest men in Sing Sing, where he was sent for bigamy and forgery. (As if it were *his* fault that the rich widows all married him and handed over their checkbooks.) My father blamed my size on my mother's Uncle Willie, who, from my child's perspective, was nine feet tall and weighed eleven pounds (unless he'd just had his shock treatments, when his weight went down to ten) and my mother's Irishness. Specifically, he blamed her mother, whom he referred to as "Sadie Two Chops," for when Nana was running the table, nobody got away with less.

I worried so about my height; I was convinced that I would never even have a date. All the girls' magazines I devoured suggested little more than wearing flats and getting a boy to talk about himself. I listened to my mother's proud, incessant size-and-weight bulletins and felt sorry for myself. I didn't think I'd ever been a size 10 or weighed 119 pounds. As far as I knew, I started out at seven pounds six ounces and then was 145 and they were letting out my dresses. It was food for thought, all right, and while I tried to figure out what to do, on any old Thursday, in the middle of any old week, my mother or my grandmother put standing rib roast or loin of pork or a turkey on the table. For us, the only difference between Thanksgiving and any old Thursday was that on Thanksgiving, my father slipped into his red vest and carved the turkey with the World War II knife that his buddy Danny, a former GI, had found in the Philippines. On those other Thursdays, my mother and grandmother were on their own.

"Spend yer money on the table," my grandmother intoned, filling and refilling my plate, "and ye won't be spendin' it on doctors." In the same way that there are three-dog nights, there are also pound-of-butter dinners, and that was pretty much where we lived, in Heavy Cream Land, where my grandmother wouldn't know a hardened artery if it bit her on the ankle.

Beef barley soup followed by sirloin steak followed by baked macaroni and cheese or mashed potatoes followed by creamed onions and creamed carrots and creamed peas and, to top it all off, a big bowl of homemade rice pudding. With whipped cream. And they wondered why nothing fit. And not just my clothes—neither my Mickey Mouse ears nor my Daniel Boone cap stayed on my head. My mother and my grandmother's solution was to drag me off periodically to Stan's of Hollywood on 37th Avenue to get my hair "thinned." (If only it were that easy for the rest of me.)

Well, calves' livers with onions and bacon to all that.

But when the Irish tongue stops cutting, when the mickey slips on a skinny-girl banana peel and falls away, then the Irish tongue—the mother tongue—paints with a word brush, and a big chubby girl imagines herself to be not only beautiful, but skinny, wearing the long-ago clothes her thin mother so lovingly describes, drawn back in time to her mother's old life.

Mom told me all about the white piqué dress with the cinched waist, and the red "wedge" sandals that she wore to William's Lake, where Eddie Coverly asked her to be his girl, before he dumped her for the shapely and beautiful Estelle. Then Mom described the camel-colored satin dress with matching peplum, the brown straw hat, the alligator-leather, ankle-strap shoes she was wearing when, years later, she ran into a round and balding Eddie Coverly—with the by-then-dumpy Estelle—on the subway. (Eddie Coverly, eat your heart out.)

Then my mother moved on to the black and white shantung silk off-the-shoulder dress and the black peau de soie pumps she wore the night Bob Gordon (the boss who was not only divorced but twice her age) took her to the Rainbow Room and asked her to marry him. She shook her head sadly when she described for me the pink and white shoulder-padded suit she wore to Central Park, where she told Mr. Gordon that her parents had forced her to say no.

But what I longed to see most was the purple and blue flowered rayon dress with the sweetheart neckline that Mom had worn to the party where she met my "gorgeous" father.

"I'll never understand what your father saw in a plain girl like me," Mom said with a sigh, and I felt as if she'd dumped a pail of cold water over my head. I loved my mother's face, her freckled cheek cooling my fevered one, her lifelong habit of biting the inside of her cheek, as if she were trying not to laugh.

My father might have been "gorgeous," but how his cheek felt pressed to mine was something I'd never find out.

"He was the handsomest man I ever laid eyes on," my mother said, so besotted with my father's looks that when he died, she looked into his casket and said he didn't look a thing like himself. After the first viewing, she unsuccessfully begged the undertaker to change his suit, for gray never *was* his color.

* * *

Though my mother expressly forbade me to go on the milk-and-soup diet, she didn't know how to dress me and I didn't know how to dress myself, for nothing fit. The unlined, red-wool leggings I wore underneath my let-out Sunday dresses were not only too tight, but too short, and forced me to walk like Groucho Marx. Though nylon stockings were part of my grade-school uniform, the blue-and-white garter belt I wore was useless. Stretched to the limit, either the garters snapped open or the elastic broke. Which was the case the day my mother was out somewhere and Sister Dolorita sent me home to my grandmother and told me not to come back "without proper undergarments." All my grandmother had was a ball of blue yarn, which I tied around my stockinged legs like a pair of tourniquets. Like high school boys who join the Marines for the uniform, I joined the Girl Scouts for the knee socks.

Finally, my mother took me to the Miss Chubbette department of Roaman's Department Store for the Large and Lovely, where there were old-lady dresses with detachable collars like the ones my old teacher, the semi-petrified Miss Hettis, wore, and where, in the dressing room, I stepped on a pin. To get the waist to fit properly meant that I needed a dress that was approximately forty feet long. My mother held the dresses up against me, and when the fabric pooled around both of our ankles, she said, "I'll just take it up a hem or two," as if I hadn't once seen her sew a button onto my father's shirt *and* her housecoat.

Like most kids, I feared monsters in my closet, but unlike those of most kids, my monsters were on hangers. Waistbands with sharp little teeth; tight corduroy pants that chafed my soft inner thighs; Easter hats with elastic bands that sunk into my neck like fossils. (Never mind all those "middle-aged-man" jokes. I *invented* the armpit belt.)

Mine was a difficult childhood of safety pins, straight pins, Scotch tape, blue yarn, runty little "business sheer" stockings, and, if I were lucky, one dependable garter. After the garter belt fiasco, my mother's friend Kay met me at the subway, leaned over the turnstile, and, as if it were contraband, handed me a big envelope with a black rubber girdle inside. The girdle was so tight that I wondered why Saint Perpetua bothered guiding a Roman soldier's sword to her throat. If it were torture she was looking for, a rubber girdle would have done the trick—and been a lot less messy.

When I was about fourteen, I took matters into my own hands. I saved my baby-sitting money, and when I was in

Mishkin's Drugs, buying Miss Clairol "Copper Penny" for my mother, I bought my very first can of Metrecal, which tasted something like Kaopectate, only maybe not so nice, and I drank it from a brown paper bag, like a wino, on the street. (Father McGinty, if you're still alive, I'm so sorry for dropping that glass bottle of hair dye on the floor of the confessional, and for running like hell when you stood up, slipped in it, fell through the purple velvet curtains, and then smashed your head on the church's marble floor.)

Kids had a lot of freedom in those days, and I developed a routine. Whenever I had enough money, I bought Metrecal, and then I went next door to Jack La Lanne's and "tried out" the machines. (No thanks, I'm just looking.) And it didn't work. I didn't lose an ounce. The weight seemed as impossible to lose as the height. I accepted that there was to be no transformation for me, no release of my inner Laura Petrie. At the Friday night church dances, where I sat at a table in the corner, boys who approached and asked me to dance were lost in my shadow the minute I stood up. Sometimes they just turned around and walked away. It was the oddest thing: The shortest boys and, later, the shortest men, although they came up only to my chin, all claimed to be five-foot-ten, the height equivalent of "two beers." It was humiliating to be so tall. At the hairdresser's, or the doctor's, or the dentist's, my wide shoulders formed a natural shelf for any dangling male parts.

I met my first serious boyfriend at a school dance. I was sixteen and he was nineteen. I'd like to say that our eyes met across a crowded room, but that goes without saying. The truth was that both of our heads were caught up in the same garland hanging over a door. We were two trees in a room full of bushes. Especially me—and with a knee-length panty girdle, a long-line bra, contact lenses, false eyelashes, and an artificial chignon, I was a human topiary, not so much dressed as "arranged." He was handsome, he was dark, but mostly, he was taller than I was. Reader, I married him.

Do I regret marrying so young, being pregnant at twenty? Not on your life. Morning sickness didn't bother me; I laughed off Braxton Hicks contractions. And almost falling out of the bedroom window with the wet bedspread I was trying to hang on the clothesline outside—well, I didn't bat an eye. Waiting for my very tall son to be born was the happiest time in my life. I could eat whatever I wanted, and everything I wore fit.

But after the baby was born, and another son right after that, I was back in the thick of it. I joined Weight Watchers four thousand times, weighing and measuring food, and the few pounds I'd lose, I'd put back on. I did Atkins, I did grapefruit, I did cabbage soup. Some of it worked, though not for long. One summer, my friend Susan and I joined a twelve-step program modeled after AA, where people admitted that they were powerless over food, and we lost weight. But then, after one meeting when a woman confessed to eating a box of tea bags, and after another meeting when someone fessed up to eating the dessert page of *Woman's Day*, Susan and I left and went shopping. (By Thanksgiving, our earrings were all that fit.)

That was the year I decided I'd had enough and would never go on a diet again.

I regret—oh, how I regret—wasting so many of those precious years, all that rich and limited energy, all the time that's now gone for good. I wonder what I missed while I was at weight-loss meetings, or counting "points," or staring at numbers on a scale. My 119-pound mother is gone now, along with my father, the dandy, and my younger brother. My younger sister has had cancer twice. All that worry about my waist was simply that: a waste. Living well is not the best revenge. Living—just plain living—is the gold.

I haven't worried about my weight in many, many years, but while I wasn't paying attention, the strangest thing happened.

I got thin.

What I Gave Up

Ellen Sussman

1989: C5/C6 and the End of My Life as a Killer Tennis Player

My father built a backboard in the yard of our small house when I was a kid. I had never heard of anyone who had a backboard. Even now, years later, I can't really say he was ahead of his time, but he wanted me to train to become a tennis champion, and so every afternoon after school, I hit an hour's worth of forehands against that backboard.

I was small and strong and determined. Friends would ask me, "Don't you hate it, the way he pushes you, the way he drills you every day?" I loved it. I loved the power I felt when I smashed the ball as hard as I could against the board and it came back at me just as hard and fast. I loved my sense of speed and agility as I lunged and sidestepped and found myself in just the right place for the next wallop.

My dad and my backboard served me well. By the time I was fourteen, I played tennis tournaments in the mid-Atlantic states and won most of my games, not with finesse or smarts, but with brute athleticism. My body worked, all of my taut muscles firing, to deliver a cross-court smash that would astonish my white-skirted, ponytailed opponent expecting a long, lovely rally. I didn't rally; I put the ball away. Over and over again.

I played varsity high school tennis and varsity college tennis and I kept my body strong and well tuned. I lived in my body, in a way that I think many girls never learn to, loving my lean muscles and knowing what they could do, where they could take me. I loved all things physical—sex, for instance—because of how highly attuned I was to the pleasures that my body afforded me.

When I hit my twenties, two roadblocks interrupted my spirited ride. After college, I couldn't make the switch to tennis as a social sport. I hated myself if I played badly. I hated my partner if she played badly. And I hated all these ugly emotions that would surface as soon as I stepped onto the court. Something had happened to me on the way to becoming a girl jock. It wasn't that I had to win—I had to play well; I had to perform. If someone was better and beat me fairly, that was just fine. But if I didn't play at the top of my game, I was miserable. Beyond miserable—I plunged into black moods that seemed to divert all that wild sports energy into grumbling and cursing and self-loathing. It was more than just a game if I played poorly; it was as if my body had failed me.

And then my body did fail me. One day, in my early thirties, I met a male friend at the tennis club for an early-morning game. We rallied for a few minutes, warming up our bodies in the cool air, waking up our muscles, getting ready for the tough game ahead. I hit a driving forehand and moved up to the net, a position I liked to command, if only because no one expected a woman to face up to hard-hitting men at the net. My opponent walloped a searing backhand at me. My instincts were fast and sharp; my arm shot out, the sweet spot of my racket pounced on the ball, and a terrible pain shot up my neck. I stumbled, blinking against the intense white pain. "I'm fine," I assured my friend. "Let's play." I played on.

By the next day, I was undone by the acute discomfort. Hot, bright, laser-sharp jolts of pain traveled down my left arm, my playing arm. Within a few days, I was headed to the hospital for spinal fusion—a disk had ruptured in my cervical spine.

During the course of a few months, I healed. But my surgeon told me that my serious tennis-playing days were over. I wouldn't be able to hit an overhead (no looking up), a serve (ditto), or a smash. And what good is my game without a smash?

1996: C6/C7 and the End of My Life as a Runner

My body needed a sport the way most people need coffee in the morning. I took up running. I was a slow runner. I thought, *This isn't competitive; this can't make me nuts.* Wrong. I ran faster. I kept a running log. I entered 10K races. I placed third in my age group in my second 10K race.

Most mornings, I set out for long solitary runs; my body felt fluid, strong, steady. I loved the easy rhythm of my legs, of my heart, of the thoughts in my head. I believed that my spine injury was healed, and that I had reinvented myself as a leaner, more focused athlete. When long runs felt too easy, I added hills. When hills felt too easy, I added sprints.

I was speeding up the steep slope of a mountain one day. I felt an explosion in my head, and then my eyes closed and my feet stumbled. I fell to the ground and held absolutely still, wanting whatever had just caused the extraordinary pain to disappear as instantly as it had come. The pain eased, but I was scared to move my body. *I should get help,* I thought. I moved my head carefully and scanned the trail in both directions. No one was around. I pushed myself up. No, it hurt too much, everywhere and nowhere, as if pain had become my body. I sat down again. *I'll wait till someone comes,* I thought.

No one came. I finally stood and walked cautiously down the mountain. I got into my car and drove myself to the emergency room of the nearest hospital.

Another disk in my cervical spine had ruptured.

Within a week, I had my second spinal fusion.

2006: L3/L4 and the End of Back-Bends

No more running, my surgeon told me. Your spine can't take the pounding anymore.

My body healed from my surgery, and within months I was restless. I needed to move. Try yoga, my physical therapist said. Me? Yoga? I'm a jock. I need to *move.*

I tried yoga. I'm not good at it. In fact, in most classes I'm the least flexible person in the room. You know the pose where you have your legs open in a wide V in front of you and then you lean forward until your torso lies on the floor? I can't even sit upright in that position.

I'm terrible at yoga. And that's a good thing.

I'm not used to being bad at something. In fact, I've been kind of stuck on being the best in the class. My husband could be the best in the class in yoga—he could twist himself into any kind of pretzel pose and, worst of all, he even seemed to be thinking evolved, enlightened thoughts while he was doing it! How did I know? When we came out of class and I bitched about my tight hamstrings, he would just sort of smile. How annoying. Instead of thinking Zen, I sat in yoga class day after day, week after week, thinking murderous thoughts: *Why can't I do this? Why can everyone else? Why can't the teacher help me do it right?*

That's right—day after day, week after week, year after year. I haven't quit.

It doesn't make sense. I'm not someone who likes a humbling experience. I want an A from the teacher, not a condescending smile that suggests I'll get there someday. Someday? What good is that? I want it now. Now!

I need yoga. I need to stretch my attitude as well as my body. Maybe that's what keeps me coming back for more.

And something has started to seep in during the years that I've been hauling my sore, aching muscles to the studio for yet another class. First of all, I can finally touch my toes. Amazing. It feels better than a driving forehand. And every once in a while, in a pose that I've been doing for ages—like triangle, for example—my body shifts ever so slightly and I think, *That's it.* That's *what?* That's what the pose is supposed to feel like, from the inside. Not from the outside, compared to all the other people in class, but inside me. Damn, it feels good.

Something else has changed through the past years. I used to spend much of my time in yoga class thinking about things. The novel I'm writing. The children I'm raising. The vacation I'm planning. I mean, there's so much extra time in yoga class—you hold those weird poses for so long, and then, at the end of class, you lie in shavasana, corpse pose, so what else are you supposed to do? *Be.* Not do. Not think. Not fill the space or time with busy thoughts. I didn't plan this change; it just happened to me. I suddenly experienced the stillness of a pose, the quiet of shavasana, the pause between breaths. And I find myself leaving class without bitching and moaning. I may even carry a secret smile on my lips!

Some yoga teachers suggest that we begin class with an intention for that class. One thing to keep in mind. One thought to fill the space. Mine is always the same: *Be here.* Some days, that's my challenge. The characters of my novel begin to speak to me during a pose. Or my daughter's lost purse sends red-hot sparks through my not-so-quiet mind. And so I remind myself: *Be here. Later, I can talk back to my characters or my daughter. Right now, the only one I have to talk to is myself.*

I got to a point where I rarely looked around in class. Yoga isn't about what anyone else is doing. I brought my own body to class, with all its tight muscles and old injuries and stubborn hamstrings. I told myself that I've got the rest of my life to live in this body. And the rest of my life to practice yoga. I told myself, *Who knows? In ten or twenty years, I may even let some of this Zen calm sneak into the rest of my life.*

And then one morning, in a class I love because the teacher is clear and calm and the studio is filled with the soft morning light that lets me move slowly into the day, I began my sun salutations. I felt my body begin to open up, to release some of its stiffness; I felt my muscles begin to stretch. My hands lifted high over my head and though I didn't look up—with a metal plate in my neck, I can't look up—I felt the expanse of that reach toward heaven. I let my arms open and began my swan dive toward the earth, my body bending at the waist. And then it happened, in a moment I've come to know too well: the flash of pain, the body-tearing blur of something going terribly wrong. I fell to the floor and lay there, waiting for the pain to pass. *No,* I thought. *Not this. I'm so good to my body now. Don't let me lose this.*

I'm now awaiting my third spinal surgery. This time, a disk in my lumbar spine degenerated, so that the bones of my spine rub against each other with no cushion between them. I'm in pain most of the day and night.

Maybe it's my lifetime of devotion to fitness that makes this debilitating illness so damn hard to take. I once expected my body to fly across the tennis court and smash an overhead. I once expected it to soar through a half-marathon. I expected it to twist into camel and fish and bow.

I'm not sure what I'll have to give up after this next surgery. I'm hoping to return to yoga classes, and that, with even more modifications, I'll still be in there, stretching my way toward enlightenment. Because success as an athlete will look different to me now. What I hope for is this: that I can live in this body without pain; that I can use it as well as I'm able to; and that my mind can accept these changes with the grace of an athlete.

Death Becomes Her

Louisa Ermelino

*"Madam Life's a piece in bloom
Death goes dogging everywhere:
She's the tenant of the room,
He's the ruffian on the stair."*
—*William Ernest Henley*

*There's a Monty Python skit that begins with a question:
"Cake? Or death?"*

My mother is dying in her bed across the street. My husband is in the hospital, defying the medical prediction that he had six months to live. It's been ten and we're still counting. Me, I'm going back and forth from the hospital to my mother's bedside to my job at a celebrity fashion magazine. Is Nicole Kidman wearing Zac Posen, and did she really buy her lasagna pan at Williams-Sonoma? Can you fax that information, please?

It's a very high-end magazine and we care about the veracity of what we print.

Today my husband wants knishes from Yonah Schimmel and chicken noodle soup from the Second Avenue Deli. I bring these things and watch him eat them. It's a very high-end hospital, but when you're coming from the outside, from the clear cold of fall, it smells bad. I'm grateful for working at a very high-end magazine and not in a hospital. I'm grateful for a lot these days. I bring my husband things that I hope will make him as happy as he can be in a hospital on borrowed time. The aides like him. They are all praying, he tells me, and asks for $20 bills to hand out, which he has always liked doing. I don't know what to talk about, so I clean things, although I hate it. He has always been so fastidious in his personal habits that I know it's hard for him in here. At home, too weak to stand at the sink to perform his ablutions, always extensive and done in private, he pulls a chair into the bathroom and soldiers on.

I go in to see my mother. Only a week ago, I came from work to find them both, my husband and my mother, in her bedroom. He had found her on the floor, gotten her back into bed. "I had a feeling about her today," he told me. "I came back to see her. I was here this afternoon and I had a feeling."

I stayed with her that night and went home at six in the morning. My husband said something was wrong and I took him to the hospital. I left for the magazine and Cameron Diaz's shoes and did you know she doesn't have such great skin?

I held my mother's hand and smoothed her brow. She couldn't talk, but I knew she could hear. I had never cleared up in my mind how I felt about the afterlife. There's a lot of ritual around death in Italian American culture. Our local funeral parlors, which numbered three in a two-block radius, are now down to one, but our undertaker, Peter DeLuca, knows how to do it right. He visits the senior citizens' center in the basement of the church to assure the ancient ones that he knows how to do it right.

I'm clear on the fact that my mother wants to wear a short dress (not one of those tulle gowns they sell you last minute in the funeral parlor) and have a fully open coffin—she wants her legs to show. She's always had good legs. (Half-open coffins are cheaper, and you don't have to wear stockings and shoes.) She's had her outfit picked out for years. So many years, in fact, that the chosen dress went out of style and we had to start all over again. She decided on the dress she wore to her only grandson's wedding, the grandson she insists she doesn't favor, but the five granddaughters know better. My mother has always favored boys. Did I mention I have a brother?

Beige satin dress, lace at the bodice, matching shoes, all put away in tissue paper. She has told me where everything is at least once a week, whenever the conversation turns to who has died (often) and what the corpse was wearing at the last wake she went to (also often). For music, she wants "Ave Maria" and "Amazing Grace" (that Protestant song that was let into the Catholic canon I'm not sure when).

But what about the afterlife? All I had was this vague Buddhist/animist/humanist idea that I'd cobbled together, once I'd "left" the church after a priest referred to my fourteen-year-old self as an "occasion of sin."

Now my mother, this woman I've loved my whole life, is leaving me. To go where? Heaven? Might all those St. Peter jokes about the pearly gates be true?

St. Peter greets you at the gate and invites you in for dinner. He serves you tea and toast. Wait a minute, you say. Tea and toast? This is heaven?

I know, St. Peter says, but it just doesn't pay to cook for two. . . .

I hold her hand and I have a vision. There's the porcelain table set in concrete under the grape arbor at my grandparents' house on Long Island. Everyone is there—my father, my mother's three sisters. It's summer and there's a breeze; it's cool under the grape arbor. My mother's sisters are all in flowered housedresses, and my Aunt Rae is coming out of the house, kicking open the screen door with her foot because in her arms she's carrying a huge bowl of spaghetti, spaghetti with gravy, sausage, and meatballs made with pignoli and raisins. I lean over my mother and I tell her what I see. "They're waiting for you," I tell her. "They are all there waiting for you. They won't start eating without you."

And I'm convinced. I know that this is where she's going, back to the people she's loved and lost, back to the good times. And I tell her that if she wants, my father will come get her, pick her up in the roadster, and she can be fifteen again and wear the coat he bought her to meet his family, the green wool coat with the fox collar, and the cloche hat.

But she won't go. She won't leave. My brother is in Europe. She's not leaving, I realize, without saying goodbye to her son. The others will have to wait.

* * *

I go to see my husband in the hospital every day. I leave work early. The doctor says he has to stay until a certain something happens. I can't stand the hospital. I can't stand the smell. I can't stand the table on wheels that goes over the bed, and the IV dangling and the hospital gowns that I sneak into the closet and take out when no one is looking, also blankets and other things, so that he can have them changed constantly, because . . . did I tell you how fastidious my husband is?

There's a crisis, and they rush him into surgery and then to the intensive care unit. The nurse asks me if he has a living will, and that I should get it. She says I should tell my children to come. I am surprised when she says this, but I listen. We can see him fifteen minutes every hour. The waiting room has a Coke machine. There are other families there and there are people wailing in the halls, and every time we go inside for our fifteen minutes, we see another empty bed. My mother is dying. My husband is dying. That might be Armani that Nicole Kidman is wearing. There's no more Diet Coke in the machine. My husband opens his eyes and decides not to die just then.

* * *

My brother comes home. I tell him to let our mother go. He says he can't, and he sits with her for a day and a night. He sits in the chair in the living room, where he always sits when he comes to see her. In the morning, he lets her go . . . to

Long Island, to eat spaghetti under the grape arbor with her husband and her sisters.

I take the dress and the shoes out of the closet. She needs underwear. I buy her a $200 pink lace bra. My brother and I go to the funeral home to see Peter DeLuca, and we take the elevator to the basement to look at coffins. We are having a good time. We pick out a beautiful, solid mahogany coffin with brass hardware. It's so beautiful, I want one for myself.

My mother is old. She's lived in this neighborhood her whole life. The dream in this neighborhood is to have many people at your wake and many flowers. It's a sign you were beloved, cherished, respected. I worry that she has lived too old for all of this. Who's left to fill the funeral parlor with flowers? Who will come to show she's beloved?

The funeral parlor has two rooms: a front room and a back room. One is bigger than the other. Not everyone needs a big room. Not everyone is beloved, cherished, respected.

My mother's wake takes over the whole funeral parlor. We are lucky, Peter tells us, that no one else has died this week, because we need both rooms. There are flowers everywhere. There are people everywhere. All afternoon and all night for two days, they come and go. My mother is having a wake to beat the band. She was almost ninety years old. She is wearing her beautiful dress and her $200 bra, and her lovely legs and satin shoes are showing beneath the chiffon hem of her dress . . . and the coffin. Did I tell you the coffin was so beautiful that I wanted one for myself?

I dig out all my beautiful black clothes. Cashmere pants and high-heeled boots; uneven-hemmed skirts and blouses with illusion net for sleeves. I line my eyes and paint my mouth for the funeral Mass. I walk up the church aisle and give a eulogy. I say my mother always believed that everyone loved her, and after this I believe it, too.

And we go in limousines to Calvary Cemetery, to the grave my father had bought many years before he needed it. There's room for six bodies in there, and the double granite headstone has our family name carved into the top in bold letters. My mother talked about the grave, too. She wanted to go side by side with my father. Don't forget, she would always say, side by side.

I'm high after the funeral. The good death, the perfect funeral, but it isn't over for me yet.

*   *   *

My husband loved my mother. He saw her every day. He talked about not knowing what he would do when she wasn't there anymore, when he couldn't stop by her house, any time of the day, to eat a banana, to take a hard candy, a glass of water, use the bathroom. She lived on the ground floor. Everyone in the family had a key, ten of us. Ten people could open her door with their own key and take one of the bananas in the fruit bowl on her counter.

Now she had died, and he couldn't even go to her funeral. I don't remember if this upset him, or if he was too preoccupied with his own struggle. I don't remember talking to him about her dying, about my vision. To be honest, I don't really remember the smell of the hospital or exactly what I did there. Not even like childbirth. I can tell you the story about childbirth, but I can't tell you much about this. I don't even know if the facts are straight, the sequence of events. It's confused. I just got myself from place to place.

My husband wanted to come home. I called the doctor, who told me I was negative and unhelpful, and that we had to make a decision to keep trying or to go into hospice.

My husband came home. He said he wanted to try whatever they were promising. We made an appointment to go back to see the doctor in his office. The doctor who had said six months was now trying. My husband had bought him lavender socks when he had laughed at my husband's pink ones.

Every week in that doctor's waiting room, people disappeared. My husband and I would joke about how long the guy at the end of the couch had left. We'd elbow each other at the signs we had learned that meant someone was on the way out. The color, the bloat, the walk. Do I look that bad? my husband would say, and I would say No, you look good. You look like you will live forever.

I cut a small cartoon out of *The Wall Street Journal*. It was of a little grim reaper, his robe dragging on the floor. He was standing on a stoop, and a man was opening the door, and the line was: "Somehow I thought you'd be taller." I wanted my husband to welcome death, to stop struggling, to stop suffering, but I couldn't put myself in his shoes. I was healthy and very much alive. I was one to talk.

* * *

The day of trying came, and my husband said he couldn't. He could not get up and get dressed (fastidiously, you'll remember), and go down those many flights of steps that are our apartment and into the street and into that office, and be the guy on the end of the couch. I wanted to try, he said, for you, for the kids, but I just can't.

I called hospice and the dying went into full gear. It's wonderful, the attention you get when you're dying, the attention you cannot have when your life is still open-ended. Suddenly, there are all these people who care about you, your comfort, your well-being. They love you. They travel great distances to see you, they bring you presents, they let you talk, they stay late, they want to be near you.

* * *

We always worried about all those stairs, my husband and I. What would happen when we got old, when we got sick, broke a leg, a hip? Stairs . . . stairs. . . .

And in the end, it was about the stairs. It was the stairs that made my husband decide to stop trying. The stairs decided for him. I love those stairs and I'm not afraid of them anymore. I even imagine living out my life on the top floor, never going out because of the stairs, like a mad old woman in the attic.

My husband lived six weeks. I bought him cashmere sweaters and fur-lined slippers. The nurse came, the doctor came, the priest came, the minister came, the social worker came, his brother and sister came. Ariane and Ruby and Lucy came to stay. Lucy brought him a cat that he said he didn't want, but he lay with it day after day and called it "my buddy." Genny came, and Gianni and Matteo and Sara and Leo. Kate came. She brought cat toys.

We drank Moët & Chandon and ate Iranian caviar with hard-boiled eggs. We ate trays of lasagna and artichokes as big as a baby's head, stuffed with egg and bread crumbs and parmesan cheese.

Thanksgiving morning, my husband couldn't get up and he stayed in bed. I said something to the nurse about Christmas, and she said he wouldn't be there at Christmas. She said it wouldn't be long. She said it was close, but I didn't see it. Can you see death coming? We sat around the bed, all of us women and that cat. We gave him morphine with an eyedropper, and ice chips laced with vodka.

I slept next to him, and in the morning I was stunned that he was still alive, warm and lying next to me. I was amazed that he had survived the night, but I knew he was very close to Hades. He might already be on that boat. Did he have the fare?

We gathered around the bed, all of us women and that cat.

*   *   *

When I was a little girl, living in a tenement down the street, a neighbor came to the door to ask my mother to come upstairs, because the woman's mother had just died. My mother took me with her rather than leaving me behind alone. Have I told you how much I loved my mother? We went upstairs and my mother closed the dead woman's eyes. I still remember the gesture: She used two fingers, her index and third on her right hand, and closed the woman's eyes. Then she took a white handkerchief and tied it around the old woman's head to keep her mouth closed so it wouldn't freeze in an open position, because your mouth goes slack when you die. I learned that standing next to my mother. I remember the old woman in the bed, propped up against pillows, looking like a cartoon character with a toothache.

*　*　*

There was the death rattle. It is a rattle and it lasts a long time. When it stopped, I lay against my husband's body. I could feel him going cold. I had promised him I would wash him. I had promised to have him wrapped in a sheet. I had promised that he would not have a wake, that he would not be carelessly dressed (have I told you how fastidious my husband was?), that he would be in a plain pine box, and that he would be cremated. I promised that if I married a hundred times more, it would be his ashes that would be put in my coffin.

I called the undertaker and I realized that undertakers come when you call. You don't have to wait until morning or leave a message on an answering machine. Things move smoothly around death.

They took the body, carried it down all those stairs. We huddled, the girls and I, in another room. We did not want to see this indignity, his body being removed and carried down the stairs. I think they used a stretcher. I remember my mother telling how they took my grandfather's body down the stairs in a basket. How does a body fit in a basket?

*　*　*

My husband is dead and I am a widow, the survivor, the star. But there's no wake. I cannot be the star. I cannot dress carefully in black and sit in the big chair in the front row of the big room in the funeral parlor and clutch a linen handkerchief with which to wipe my tears. Did I tell you my husband didn't want a wake?

There was a Mass, and I carefully chose my black clothes and did my hair and applied lipstick and lined my eyes in black. I read the eulogy from the pulpit, in the same spot where I had stood only six weeks before. I didn't cry. I didn't falter. I was elegant. I felt beautiful and powerful and very alive. Outside, the world was Technicolor. Everything I touched felt electric.

I have a vision. My mother is at the stove; my husband is at the kitchen table. The sun is coming in the window. She is making him something to eat.

Cake, please. . . .

My Mother's Body Image, My Self

Sara Nelson

I have a new boyfriend. He is very nice and very sexy. He likes me. In the course of the seven months that we have been together, here are some of the words he has used to describe my body: "curvy," "round," "sexy," "generous," and once, in a moment of passion, "lush." I think once he even described me as "Rubenesque."

That's how many times I have wanted to kill him.

First, some basics. I'm about five-foot-nine. My weight varies from 140-ish to—and I'll tell you this, but I'm doing so only because I'm on the low end these days—155-ish. I've been a size 8 (6 in expensive clothes) to a size 10 (12 in the cheapest). I have never resembled the fat lady in the circus, even on my worst days. But—and here is the part that tortures me always—I have *never* looked even vaguely like Kate Moss. *A body like a hanger?* The kind loved by all those gay fashion designers who like girls to look like boys? No, never me. Not even when I weighed in, for one and a half days in my near-anorexic midtwenties, at 122. I am, after all, curvy, round, generous, just like the man said.

* * *

I am twelve years old and at my yearly appointment at the pediatrician's office. This is in the days before twelve-year-olds are routinely routed to the gynecologist, and besides, this is small-town Pennsylvania. My mother, June, has brought me to see Dr. Klein, the kids' doctor whom everybody, especially every Jewish body, has claimed as her personal physician for at least one generation.

"Hop up on the scale," he tells me. I do as I'm told.

"One hundred thirty-five pounds," he announces to the nurse and to my mother, who's in the room with me.

Do I imagine it, or does my mother grimace? "That's what I weighed when I got married," she tells me later.

* * *

For as long as I can remember, the world saw me as a junior clone of my mother, a mini-her, in looks primarily, but also in personality. I can remember being as young as perhaps five and my father calling me "Junie Junior," with great affection, of course. The joke around our house was that I couldn't go anywhere in our smallish town without some adult, some stranger, walking up to me and saying, "You must be June Nelson's daughter." Never mind that when I look at photos of myself from that age and compare them to hers at the

same age—or look at my fifty-year-old self next to pictures
of her fifty-year-old self—I see only the most basic, police-
blotter similarities: very dark hair, almond eyes, pale skin. She
is much rounder faced than I am. Now that my coloring has
faded a bit, I can see that I actually look more like my father.

But there was no bigger mama's girl than I. My mother
and I shared many interests, but whether that was nature or
nurture, I couldn't say. An avid reader and frustrated writer, she
taught me to care about what she cared about, and I was happy
to learn. My mother was a Francophile; I started studying the
language in second grade. She liked to play bridge; I can still
remember the agonizing after-dinner sessions during which she
and my father tried to teach me, and which usually ended up in
screaming matches that sent me slamming off to my room.

And shopping. Oh, yes, then there was the shopping.
Hours and days and weekends we spent at the Kiddie Shoppe,
buying outfits I passionately declared that I *needed*—outfits
that she would instruct me to carry stealthily up the back
stairs so that Daddy wouldn't see how many packages we
had. Even so, a few hours later, she'd send me back upstairs
to put them on and model for my father.

In my prepubescence, shopping with my mother was
pretty fantastic. They were great clothes, and it never
occurred to me at the time that my mother was having me
do all the things she couldn't do, that she was projecting her
dashed hopes for herself onto me. At fifty, my mother was
in the midst of losing the body-image battle she'd fought
all her life. After four children—and forty extra pounds
("Ten for each kid," she'd say)—she was definitely heavy,

but nowhere near as heavy as she thought she was, as she felt. Soon, I would come to hear all about it. The way she saw it, she was almost the fat lady in the circus: heavy, obese, gross. You couldn't tell her—and I wouldn't have known how to— that she was more Margaret Dumont in the Marx brothers' movies: heavy, regal, powerful, formidable. I remember once taking a candid Polaroid of her as she and my father walked across the lawn for my brother's high school graduation. When June saw it, her face turned grim and she walked on ahead. "Why is Mom mad?" I asked my father. His reply was enigmatic and somehow accusatory: "Why do you think?"

*   *   *

To say that body image was an issue in our house is an understatement akin to saying that there have been some trust problems in business and government of late. We were "big people," most of us, tall and big-boned and, well, fleshy. And I hit adolescence in the very late '60s, Twiggy's time. We were definitely not Twiggys. I was four inches taller than all of my friends and probably forty pounds heavier—not off the charts, but noticeably different . . . to everyone but my mother. Never mind that I look at pictures of myself from that time and see a sturdy girl, some baby fat for sure, but hardly extreme, even at my beefiest. How people looked—which was simply code for how their bodies looked—was the most important thing. Yes, it was important to do well in school, to be polite, to be kind, to count your blessings. But if you didn't look "right," well, you could just forget about peace.

And it simply wasn't possible to resemble my mother, or me, and look, in Nelsonese, "good." This was a time before "self-improvement" became a job description for American culture, but it was also a time before educated people routinely psychotherapized that culture. It would never have occurred to us at 36 Butler Street that we were being "tyrannized" by a "looks-ish" environment, that there was anything wrong with staring at your thirteen-year-old self and finding it lacking. Or, more accurately, overflowing.

* * *

By the time I was in high school, those shopping trips with my mother had turned sinister. Would this skirt show the world the truth about my "can," as my mother so uncharacteristically and vulgarly called it? (My butt was, and is, fleshy.) A good outfit, on the other hand, was pronounced "flattering," which always implied to me that it hid, not celebrated, some offending part. As for breasts, well, I had 'em, and nobody ever said much about them, except when the fabric of a dress pulled across them, and that was definitely not a plus.

I know other women my age who grew up in similar environments, of course, although when I've met their mothers, the women have turned out to be skinny-starved, Chanel-clad moms who worried that their non-hangerlike daughters would not enjoy the advantages that their angularity had brought them. (There were no Chanel suits for the size 14s, after all.) Those daughters always seemed angry, and they fought back by becoming anorectics or exercise-holics or sometimes purposely, purposefully fat. I was not angry, at least not then—I loved my mother. I wanted to be close to her, and if that meant worrying, obsessing over how we both looked, how alike we were, well, to my mind that was okay. Our weight and body obsession was what connected us. It was something we could share. "Hi, how's your weight?" was not an unusual way for her to start a letter to me at camp, nor was it odd for me to reply readily with specifics.

"I saw Sandy K. on the street today," I'd announce at dinner. "Oh, yes?" she'd ask, eyes narrowing as she remembered my childhood nemesis, who everyone in town thought was a great beauty but who we, my mother and I, had declared a bit too zaftig for our taste. "Did she get fat?" Who looked good, who looked bad, who'd put on weight, who'd gotten thin—these topics were our conversational currency. And we were definitely free spenders.

When my adolescent rebellion came, it was the same as everybody else's: I withdrew from the parental conversation. But I didn't blimp up or starve down. I still weighed myself obsessively many times a day; I still could run a tab of all the calories I'd consumed in the previous week; I still counted dimples on my thighs and snuck looks at other girls' inevitably smoother ones in gym class, but I didn't talk about it anymore, least of all to my mother. Now, when I'd come home from boarding school for vacation and mention an old friend I was seeing, she'd still ask, "How does she look?" but I'd refuse to answer. "I didn't notice," I'd say (lie). Or, when I was feeling strident, "Who cares?"

But the imprint remained. A therapist I had been seeing said once that it hardly mattered that my mother and I didn't discuss our bodies anymore. I'd been "vaccinated" with the body-image disease, she said, and the virus lived inside me, like herpes. With any stress, it would erupt. And since I'd never really learned how to express unhappiness or pain or fear or frustration in any other way, a bad grade or a bad breakup would manifest itself as a body-image breakdown. Unlike those people who run around with free-floating anger, looking for a place to put it, I had a huge, deep, unfillable vat right in front of me all the time: I could blame my body. For years, my same therapist would insist that I couldn't be weeping in her office because I'd gained an actual five pounds; it had to be something else. Was I sure I wasn't upset that my boyfriend had left me or my father had died? Well, of course I was, I'd reply. But it would all be more manageable if I weren't so damn fat.

*   *   *

There's a woman I know through business, a woman a decade older than I and, objectively, a whole lot bigger and maybe less attractive than I am at my worst. I see her often at business functions, at meetings, in more social situations. I don't know her well, but I admire her. This woman—let's call her Joan— thinks and acts like a Beauty. She wears beautiful, expensive clothes; she flicks her long hair; she flirts with all men, not just the much younger, attractive boyfriend with whom she lives. She's a powerful woman in the world in which we travel, it's true, but her real power is in her: She thinks she's pretty great.

People we know in common inevitably complain that she's full of herself, that she has become ridiculous, a caricature, a woman who acts like a girl, mutton dressed as a lamb. But I think differently. I think she must have had a fabulous mother, someone who told her every day and in a million ways that she was beautiful. I imagine that her adolescent dressing-room scenes were a whole lot different from mine. "Oh, Joanie, you look so good in everything," I can hear the mother saying. "You're gorgeous."

*   *   *

I sometimes wish I had had this kind of mother, a woman so secure in her own self-image that she didn't need to visit her anxieties upon her daughter. (I've since met Joan's mother. No skinny, Chanel-clad socialite, she is still extraordinarily beautiful and confident in her eighties.) Likewise, I envy the twentysomethings I see in the stores and markets near where I now live: normal-size girls in low-slung jeans, with bare midriffs often accentuated by enormous tattoos. And sometimes they're not even normal size. In case you haven't heard, we have an epidemic of obesity in this country, and some of these girls should probably be worried about their weight and their bodies, not showing off their excess flesh so proudly. When I was their age, I was taking to my bed because I'd tipped the scales that morning at 125 1/2. But they're proud, and somebody taught them to be.

*   *   *

My mother taught me plenty that was good and healthy. How to be generous, for example, and how to be kind, at least to others. She taught me well about books, and about friendship, and even (despite my recent divorce) about love. What she didn't teach me, because she couldn't, was how to give myself a break, to accept and celebrate what wasn't so bad in the first place. By now we've both grown up enough to be able to joke about it—about the juice fasts we used to go on together, about the ripped photographs, even about those dressing-room adventures. She still doesn't quite get why all our obsessing was wrong, and she'll sometimes suggest that she did me a favor after all. "If it weren't for those days," she says, "you wouldn't be as thin as you are."

*   *   *

It's Thanksgiving weekend and I'm visiting my mother, who's eighty-eight now and lives mostly in a wheelchair. But she is still very lucid and, as always, we talk. How is my job going? Did I vote? What's going on with my love life? She never says a word about how I look, unless it's to remark that my hair or teeth look beautiful, or that she likes my style. I don't tell her, even now, that I diet for a few days before I'm due to visit her because I know she'll be looking at me. I also don't tell her that, when I'm staying with her, I try to get up before she does every morning, so that I can sneak into the bathroom and weigh myself on her scale—whether to ease my mind or make myself crazy, I still don't know. My mother has learned, after years of my silence and my tantrums and my accusations that she "made me this way," not to bring up the forbidden topic, at least not as it applies to either of us. But sometimes she can't help herself.

My twelve-year-old son, who is not with me on this particular trip, is a bit on the chubby side, and my mother worries that he's going to have social problems because of it. She frets about his "weight problem," but she also loves him for it. Like me, he has something in common with her, even if I make sure it remains an unspoken something. She is, as always, desperate to connect.

I'm desperate to connect too, though, and these last years have been a search for other topics, a reemphasis. Even after all this time, she'll still ask me how this or that old friend looks and will occasionally let slip, with some disgust, that someone we know has "gotten fat." Virtually immobile now, she has given up the body-image battle once and for all, and, while the doctors lecture her about cholesterol and heart disease, she indulges, seemingly without guilt, in Taco Bell and Three Musketeers bars. She has gotten much heavier, and her minor medical problems would probably be solved if she laid off the nachos a bit.

But I see this all as improvement: If you can't just be who you are as you approach ninety, for God's sake, when can you? Better late than never, I say, and I wonder if at some point I too will begin to let this all go. She almost has, but then, old ways die hard. As I was wheeling her into a movie theater yesterday, I had to squeeze myself in between her chair and the wall. As we settled in, she turned and looked back at me. "It's a good thing you're so thin," she said.

Will it surprise you to hear that that one little comment made my whole day?

Heavy Lifting
Sally Terrell

March 1992

"Fanelli on the platform. Miller on deck. Terrell in the hole."
An announcer is calling the next three competitors at the
Olympic Weightlifting Nationals in Baton Rouge, Louisiana. We
are among the top lifters in the country in our weight class (60
kilograms, or 132 pounds), based on our qualifying totals and
performances in regional meets.

I'm standing on the warm-up platform, a red blanket draped
over my shoulders, holding a thermos of ginseng tea, which I
sip between sets. I've logged in more than three hundred hours
of workouts during the past year to prepare for the next three
minutes. One of two things will happen: Either I will successfully
hoist the barbell over my head, or I will not. The judges will
press the white light (a good lift) or the red one (no lift). In a
weightlifting competition, it's that simple.

At the back of the large fitness center converted for this event
is a broad platform over which hangs a banner: USA WEIGHTLIFTING

NATIONALS, 1992. Three judges sit in a semicircle at the front of the stage, their backs to the audience, where they observe each attempt and make sure lifters do not "press out" the bar with their arms or touch elbows to thighs. When the lifter has legally completed the lift and has held the finish for the prescribed time, the judges give the electronic signal. About 150 people are sitting in the audience, and another 50 or 60 are standing or walking about in the rear. It's one thing to make lifts in the basement weight room of my coach's physical therapy office; it's quite another to do it in front of 200 people.

February 1991

I was standing before a large wooden box that was perhaps three feet tall. I had one last set, which meant jumping up and onto the box fifteen times while wearing a twenty-pound weighted vest. This exercise strengthens the hip flexors and gluteal muscles for faster response time while in the front squat. My right leg was wrapped in ice, which was secured tightly with an Ace bandage protecting a two-inch gash on my shin, the result of a momentary lapse of concentration during the previous set. My tights were soaked in blood below the cut, which needed stitches.

I had already cried, taken a drink of water, and received words of encouragement from Marc, my coach. I knew he expected me to do the last set; I knew I would do it because I was no wimp. I also knew that I wouldn't get stitches because I *wanted* the scar, one that would later fade into an opaque triangle, joining numerous other body marks representing a lifetime of traumas—in this case, my impending divorce. Early on, I had developed a habit of punishing myself for things beyond my control: my parents' simultaneous institutionalizations and their eventual divorce, my first stepfather's violation of me, my dad's death from alcoholism, my mom's suicide—all before my twenty-third birthday. Scars were my proof that I had suffered and survived.

At first I was apprehensive about taking up weightlifting. Marc, who had been my strength coach in college, had convinced me to try it when I moved back to Connecticut, after my first husband and I had separated. At twenty-seven, I had a lithe runner's physique and I was worried that lifting would make me too muscular looking. After all, my predominant image of Olympic weightlifters had been shaped by images of huge Russian men sporting bad leotards, pear-shaped bodies, and an overabundance of back hair, waddling out to the lifting platform. At the same time, I was intrigued. I was a recovering cheerleader and prom queen, and what could be a more powerful statement of my reinvention than working out with a bunch of big, hairy guys in a basement gym that smelled like mildew?

About a month in, I was hooked, and I drove an hour each way into New York to train with the team, with the goal of making the nationals. (American women lifters wouldn't participate in the Olympics for another five years.)

"Tight!" Marc shouted as I wobbled, my legs two-stepping left, then back, then right. I tried to focus on the picture hanging on the wall in front of me: a younger and more svelte Marc doing this same lift at the nationals fifteen years earlier, and with four times the weight. As I thrust the bar overhead, I felt a pressure in my brain and saw a fuzzy black ring encroaching on my vision. This was the first time I had tried to jerk more than a hundred pounds, and I was about to pass out. The entire effort of lifting, squatting, and hoisting may seem superfluous, even absurd, to anyone unfamiliar with Olympic-style weightlifting. But for me, taking on this new sport—another thing to learn and master—was exhilarating and empowering.

"Okay, drop it," Marc said, and I simply let go, not knowing that I was supposed to guide the bar as it came down, allowing the rubber-coated plates to bounce from the lifting platform. He ignored my mistake and gave me a firm slap on the back. I nodded sternly, as if to say, *Damn right.*

Marc's tough-guy brand of reinforcement was important to me. Every sport I'd ever competed in—track, cross-country, soccer, and now this—was as much about gaining approval, mostly from male coaches, as it was about winning. It went back as far as my being six years old and tossing the football in the yard with my dad, a few months before he left for good. He taught me to throw a tight spiral, and each time I put the ball on the money, his sweet, slightly crooked smile told me everything was right with the world.

March 1992

"Miller on the platform. Terrell on deck. Friedman in the hole."

Miller has just missed her first clean-and-jerk attempt at 65 kilos (143 pounds), which is also my opening lift. I pace the area adjacent to the stage, where six practice platforms line the back wall. Marc comes over to recheck my knee wraps and massage my legs. I push away thoughts of my disappointing performance half an hour earlier. I had hoped to snatch 57.5 kilos (127 pounds), a lift in which the barbell is hoisted in a wide grip from floor to overhead squat in one motion, but I did only 47.5 kilos (103 pounds).

I'm dead last at the moment. I know that the clean-and-jerk—the two-part lift from floor to front squat up to standing, then overhead—is my stronger lift, so I'm hoping to gain ground. My goal is a top-ten finish.

May 1991

After four months of strength training, I had a well-defined set of trapezius muscles forming a large bump that spread out from behind my neck to each shoulder. My shoulders became squared, with a dimple separating the deltoids at the top of each arm. My lower back became hard as bedrock, and my chest—where the bar rests in the front squat—became thicker and formed a shelf above my breasts. I had to squat more than 200 pounds and dead-lift close to 250 to be competitive in the snatch and clean-and-jerk events at the nationals, and I was getting there. Whenever Marc wanted to show me how tough I'd become, he'd slap me hard, flat palmed, on those pectoral muscles. The force would send me back two or three steps, but my rock-hard chest was impervious to the blow.

The confluence of the changes in my physique and my tenuous marital status made for interesting theater. After five months of separation, I returned to Cape Cod in an attempt to save the marriage, taking my weights with me. Paul was supportive about my lifting, as he was about everything, and I took over the garage and traveled out of state to compete. That August, however, I left him for good, packing my Pontiac with six hundred pounds of barbells, plates, and collars. Whatever room was left was used for clothes and books. I had driven ten miles from the Cape, sobbing and sniffling, my cat on my lap, when I smelled burning rubber. I turned and saw smoke billowing out in a wake behind the car.

October 1991

Choosing to participate in an obscure sport, whose name and rules are unknown and confusing to most, and vaguely threatening to some, involves challenges. In most gyms, Olympic lifting is freakish, even within the idiosyncratic subculture of weightlifting. (This stigma has begun to change in recent years, as strength trainers have discovered the benefits of the Olympic style for their football-playing protégés.) There are distinct differences between bodybuilding, power lifting, and Olympic-style lifting. Bodybuilders "make muscle," lifting weights for the sole purpose of creating muscle mass and looking like the bronzed Adonis and Aphrodite on the cover of *Muscle & Fitness* magazine. Their moves follow a similar pattern of up/down, out/in, usually amplified by matching spandex, fake tans, too much makeup, and a trail of bad perfume. Power lifters are judged by the sheer amount of weight they can squat or press. Olympic lifters generally prefer ripped gray sweats and free T-shirts over spandex or muscle shirts. We make noise when we lift, and our moves are more dramatic.

Before I had my own platform at home, I trained at Gold's Gym. But I was looked at askance by the musclehead wannabes, mostly for being able to out-squat and out-grunt quite a few guys. When the spandex bunnies made it clear I wasn't welcome there, I set up a makeshift platform in the basement of my apartment: two slabs of rubber matting separated by an inch-thick sheet of plywood. Marc arrived with a forty-five-pound bar and a spare set of eight large plates, collars, and smaller metal plates. We jury-rigged a squat rack by soldering poles to car wheels. I loved the raw, unadorned look of the lifting platform and the primary colors of the spare tire–size Eleiko barbells.

As I lifted more weight, my wrists, knees, and legs hurt the way children's bones do from growing pains. I learned how to measure weights in kilos and was soon squatting well over my body weight. My wrists became thicker and stronger; I no longer tried to be graceful when I was lifting the bar. This new brand of grit and power paid dividends, as I learned to live alone for the first time in my life. I was earning a living by teaching part-time and waitressing at a high-end Hartford restaurant. I had started to sleep through the night, with all the lights off and no need for the soothing voices in the television. I even started dating a slick attorney, a regular at the restaurant, who thought I needed to be better fed.

One night, my lawyer boyfriend came over drunk and wanted to squat the 220 pounds of weight on the bar. I tried to dissuade him as he dipped under the bar and then felt perverse pleasure when he collapsed under the barbell and fell to the floor, not particularly concerned about the dust on his Armani suit. It was one more reminder that I had something to prove to the men in my life. Whether it was throwing a tighter spiral, hitting a more punishing backhand, or outkicking them at the end of a run, my physical fitness was my defense against the powerlessness my mother had exhibited with men. I later realized that it was also my attempt to protect myself from the pain of breaking up. It never worked.

September 1997

Fitness—particularly its false promise of control over our bodies and ourselves—is fickle and illusory. At least once a year I became injured because of overtraining, in part because I was using my body to get, keep, or forget some man. I couldn't find that middle ground, that place where I wasn't pushing myself too hard or recovering from an injury, physical or emotional. I missed an entire semester of teaching because of a slide tackle in a soccer game, which necessitated the insertion of a five-inch metal plate and seven screws in my ankle, eight weeks off my feet, eight more of physical therapy, and two additional surgeries. It was then, in my midthirties, that I learned that my body would not do whatever I wanted, whenever I wanted. Why did I insist on pushing myself to the point of punishment? There I was, happily building a life with my second husband, but I still couldn't slow down.

Spring 2000

After the ankle rehab and my return to the soccer field, I was more aggressive than ever. I played hard, shouting directives at my teammates, being physically aggressive with opposing players. I bought a mountain bike, started running in road races again, and trimmed down to my college weight. Whatever I was trying to work out in my head, my aging body was paying the price. At my annual physical, the nurse-practitioner took one look at the bruises on my arms and legs and asked softly, "Do you feel safe at home?"

Two years later, I cut back on soccer and joined a tennis team. I finally calmed down, and I wasn't yelling as much, but my second marriage went south. Ironically, while my husband became increasingly fanatical about working out—an attempt to stave off his midlife crisis—I found myself reducing my physical activity level to once a week. I began to make comfort food and ate enough for two, although I was living alone for the first time in twelve years. As I shoveled a second helping of beef stew into my mouth, I became aware of the psychic split I had been living with all my life. There was the little girl who survived a difficult childhood through her involvement in sports; there was the woman facing the failure of her second marriage while trying to find peace. Child and woman had been existing in a parallel space, aware of each other, but not well acquainted.

And I gained twenty pounds.

I was unhappy about my weight gain, yet the experience helped me to discover that athletics alone cannot carry me through the initial stages of the difficult, and sometimes subtle, passage of midlife. As my body began to succumb to gravity and aging, I didn't run quite as fast, my first step on the soccer field was a little slower, and my joints reminded me every morning that years of pounding had taken their toll. I began to discover a more peaceful, contented self in the silent spaces between fits of activity.

March 1992

"Sally Terrell on the platform. This is her final attempt at 72.5 kilos, 159 pounds."

My facial expression is stony and intent; I look like I'm going to hurt something. I have chalked my hands and shins. The hands need to be dry, the shins smooth, to facilitate the initial pull of the bar from the floor up the leg.

Standing in the center of the platform, five feet behind the bar, I shake out my arms and take a deep breath. I look over the heads of the judges and the audience, shaking my arms once more, and then take four deliberate steps toward the bar. I line up my feet under the bar and measure out two lengths between thumb and pinkie, getting the right spacing for my hands. Just before starting the lift, I calm my body—feet grounded firmly, hands in a loose grip, knees bent over the bar, back straight—and then I breathe in big and hold the breath as my arms become taut and my butt drops. With chest up, I pull, pull up the shin, snap the weight in the middle by jerking my back straight, and then pull up through my torso, keeping the bar as close as possible to my abdomen.

As the weight flies up, my grip loosens and my arms flip under, my body simultaneously dropping into a crouch. I catch the bar and all that weight on the muscular shelf at the top of my chest, and at that moment release the breath, shouting "Up!" followed by a loud, drawn-out "Uuuuuuuuup!" as I rise, pushing my hips out and exploding in the thighs to drive up to a standing position. There is a moment when I regroup, standing with the bar on my chest, arms underneath and elbows forward. I adjust my hands and regrip. Moment of truth. I dip slightly, keeping chest and back and hips and legs in perfect alignment, and then thrust into the split step—right leg forward, left leg back and bent—as I jerk my arms straight overhead. Over-rotate and the bar falls behind; not enough thrust and it collapses in front.

But I'm in the slot. It's overhead. I lock it in and then step my left leg forward and my right leg back to standing. White light. Good lift. "Down!" says the head judge.

Tenth place. I jump into Marc's arms offstage and receive high-fives and hugs from teammates. Making that lift was one of the most exhilarating athletic moments of my life.

November 2006

I am out for a run on a wooded trail by the Farmington River. It's an unseasonably warm November morning, with a soft, steady rain coming down. It's perfect weather for a trot, as I now call my morning runs. I am not training for a 5K, not trying to hit a minute-per-mile goal, not trying to trim down to look more fit for somebody else. I'm not sure why or how it feels so good to do this now, but I do know that, when I'm about a mile out, I can feel my breath moving in and out of me in a way I couldn't manage when I was a teenager. The rhythm of my hips and legs swinging easily beneath me seems to be part of some larger pulse that I sense in the river and among the trees.

This may be all I need to know today.

The Body Is My Land

Leora Skolkin-Smith

The Kabbalah says that we are all points at first, tiny dots isolated from the larger world. We grow into lines and start to connect with other dots, and then we are lines thickening into planes, expanding out, enlarging our form and starting point.

* * *

I remember Jerusalem. One summer afternoon of 1963, when I was eleven years old. Wet hosiery and underwear hanging in the descending sun outside on the porch, the bedroom window opened, the raised thick metal blinds still with bullet holes from the 1947 War of Independence against the British.

The lawns by the swimming pool at the King David Hotel will be green and sweet in the closing of the day, and there soon will be dishes of sherbet, curled into icy scoops and served with sugar wafer cookies to American and European tourists.

But the borders of Israel are raw: settlements of coarse land and citrus growths; artillery and rust. The air in the room is prickly with the presence of dry pine and bush that blows in from the dusty streets. The *chomaseem*, very bad weather, is on its way, unbearable heat waves that sweep the country.

It is the end of July and my mother has taken my older sister, Iris, and me back to Israel to visit my Aunt Nehama and my grandmother. I have been here four weeks.

My mother lies in her white slip in our shared bedroom with a yellow marble floor and a plain wood closet. Inside the closet's wobbly door is tacked a long mirror with handles held together by bolts that look like broken old teeth. I sleep in this room with my mother and Iris, who is already up and taking one of her endless showers in a bathroom down the hall.

I have spent a long time this siesta wondering about that closet mirror. On its glass are blotches, streaks, and finger marks that alter the reflected images. If I look into the mirror too hard, I sometimes think I'll see all the places that have populated my boyish body, like colonies of different flesh, like Israel itself and its borderless villages of disharmony: two breasts growing; my nose, which was small and shaped like the end of a spoon, suddenly thicker. It is inside my body that my center, my starting point, awaits, but I am still too young to understand what my afternoon dreams mean or to identify the soft ripple of sexual chords that my dreams sometimes arouse inside my flesh.

I pull off the bedsheets, preparing to get ready for our Friday night meal. The siesta light dims to a cool gray. I have to concentrate, shake my head and ankles. My mother is sitting on the edge of the bed, buttoning a cashmere sweater she has taken from her night table. The closet door has not yet been opened.

My aunt bursts into the room, clapping her hands as a beating order. "It's time to get dressed. Leora, get up! Iris is already in the shower. We are having the Friday night supper early, and guests are coming to eat with us!" She goes over to the closet and turns the rusted key. "Leora can wear my son's old shorts," she says to my mother, as she tries to tighten her bathrobe belt around her muscular waist.

Outside, stray cats are running from the cactus bushes into the street, where there are sounds of automobiles and motorbikes. The early moon will soon begin to travel between the invisible world, which contains my starting point, and the illuminated limestone homes.

"Love . . . is . . . a . . . many-splendored thing," the transistor radio in the bathroom suddenly blares. My sister is singing in the shower.

"Oy, Iris with this music," my mother says.

"Really, Rachel," Nehama responds. "This isn't funny. Your daughters always play rock music."

I know that Iris is smoking the cigarettes I got from Mr. Haggittee's grocery store. I also know that if only cold water comes out of the shower spout, she will scream, like she did when she saw one of our uncle's wooden legs hanging with the towels.

"You will tell Iris and Leora to dress nicely for tonight," Dota Nehama says. "They are to come to the table in their good clothes." I watch the two women, blinking so I will not fall asleep again. I don't want to be like my Aunt Nehama when I am her age, my body like this house, scorched and crusty on the outside because the sun has shone too much on its face and worn it out.

On the night table, I had left a chewed wad of pink Israeli gum. I push it loose because I have not found any fresh packages under my cot.

Dota Nehama turns her back on me. She reaches into the wooden closet and takes out some army shorts and heavy leather sandals for me to wear, putting them on a chair near my cot. She begins to search the back shelves for some sun hats. Old dresses on wire hangers block her hands. She throws the dresses to the floor. Cricket balls tumble out from behind hatboxes, and *Dr. Dolittle* storybooks fall with the balls. My aunt's arms are strong, bulging with tough muscle. A sagging pocket of underarm skin makes the bursting strength in her upper arms seem even firmer than it is.

I rouse myself from the cot, standing in my nightgown and bare feet and chewing the gum, which has begun to soften against my teeth.

"I will take the girls to Masada on Sunday," my aunt is saying. "They will learn to be Israelis."

"Oy, Nehama. Don't tell me how to raise my children. You are worse than the army," my mother quips.

Their voices are so loud, I wish I could cover my ears. I open a packet of Wash'n Dri and run the perfumed cloth over my face. The window is open and the blinds are up, letting in the heat from outside. The stronger evening breezes have not come yet.

I sometimes think this stone house is an ossuary. It is a rambling space with no boundaries and tulips on its three porches that make it smell sweet. The sediment inside the limestone bricks is worn and hard. Inside ossuaries are the bones of the departed, but at One Palmach Street, there are no bones, only framed photos on the mantel, including a picture of the lost brother no one talks about and photographs of my mother's father and her uncle.

I have found all the mirrors in this stone house. One is in the dining room, where the British shot a hole behind the painting of the Jewish settlers. Another is in the WC, where the thick stench of my sister's cigarettes stays in the air and old butts swim in the toilet. There is also a mirror in the foyer, above the steel mailbox holding letters I have written, which are waiting to be mailed to my father in America.

I don't want to see any more pictures of my mother when she was young or hear any more stories. I miss my father.

Sometimes when I look in the mirror, I feel myself losing the contours of my body. I see myself standing large and fiery like my mother, with stocky legs and thick, muscled arms. There's a feathery cuff on some of her old satin and silk dresses that hang in this closet, dresses she wore to the balls she attended with British officers. Each marriage proposal that a British or Israeli gentleman offered to her—they had to put everything in writing so her father could examine the man's intent and the future he was promising—is in the hatbox on the top closet shelf, above the stack of romance novels. My mother keeps her bottles of body washes there, too, lotions made from avocados (oval shaped, like her) and extracts of chamomile and lemon. The British soldiers came to drink port in the salon with her brothers and brought her cashmere and body washes. They let her ride in their jeeps during the hot nights as they patrolled the taken city.

I will be unable to sleep again tonight, and it could be that I am invisible and have no form. My mother will take me into her bed again. "Come," she said last night. "Nehama makes me feel bad and I am treated like I am nothing. Did you hear how she talks to me? So why did I leave Israel, if only to marry your father, who does not even call?" Her desperation quiets when she holds me close. In Israel, she has grown more careless about herself. When it is time to sleep, she is usually without undergarments, which gives a hot, wettish odor to the sheets I lie beneath with her. Last night, her hair and face creams gave off a strong, fruity smell, tempering the raw, coarse aromas that got loose from her flesh. But her strength is more muscular in its war against grief and distress than I have ever seen it, and I want to be near it, because the stone house is very cold before the sun rises and outside there is danger and soldiers are in the streets.

The bedroom has become steamy, as it has every siesta since we arrived. I feel the almond oil and the sweet, hot odor of my mother's flesh. I sense a vanishing that makes me feel like a little girl again, and there is no danger to this, I am thinking. But when I cannot push my mother off, I experience a world of sensations and feelings and I think that I will kill myself if I can't kill her. It is this feeling that I can't explain, how my mother moves through me like the faint slap of a hand, and how I can be stretched and pulled and formed invisible. I feel the hot flow of myself under the power of her body, as if I have been pulled into a magnetic field.

Yesterday Iris told me that sometimes it's as if my mother is my boyfriend, the way I let her hold me. I had a dream once that my mother turned into a man and it was how I vanished, trying to love her. I have found many topics inside the old British psychology books on the shelves in the foyer. One, called *Psychology You Can Use,* had a chapter about mothers who think their children are their own flesh, like just another lump or limb. I need to study more from the psychology books so I can talk to my father about this when I get back to America.

The bedroom door opens and my sister pads into the room, holding the transistor radio. A bath towel is around her tall body, and large drops of water slide down her long hair and from her uncovered shoulders and legs. The flesh on her naked skin is so white, she could be made of limestone, like the streets.

Iris goes to her corner of the room, where her clothes are clean and ironed. She goes outside in the early morning, after washing them, and hangs them on the clothesline on the downstairs porch where her hairdressing equipment is: pink curlers big as rocks, and jars of Dippity-do that look like Jell-O. Iris says, "Suffer for beauty, Leora" whenever she pulls me to sit on the lounge chair and tells me to pretend I am getting my hair done in a salon in Paris.

* * *

I put my hand on the strap of my nightgown and begin to pull it down, past my hips and then my calves, picking up the shorts and sun hat from where Dota Nehama laid them.

My mother checks herself in the dresser mirror, pulling her lips in to blend the lipstick into their flesh. And then she turns and looks at me. She stares a long time at me with my nightgown off, at my body. First it is a hard stare, and then her large eyes soften. "Leora has bosoms now, do you see, Nehama?" she says.

"These bosoms are not so big, Rachel," Nehama replies.

"But they are there," my mother says. "They are there now."

Was it the doorbell that suddenly rang all the way from downstairs, signaling the arrival of a guest? I will never know, but all three of them rush down the long marble steps to the foyer, leaving me alone. Only half-dressed, I know I have time, that I am safe, because the long, winding stairway is too difficult to climb. Guests are arriving: I hear them going into the salon for brandy and slivers of eggplant and olive appetizers.

I enter the closet and shut the door behind me. I pull the long string that makes the closet light up. Tattered paperbacks are piled on a shelf above the high-heeled shoes and silk dresses my mother wore when she was in the Haganah, the Jewish underground.

In these romance novels, the women are always getting "enchanted," and I know this means they are having the same ripples and wetness that my dreams bring to my body. I feel an invisible world in that closet, curling myself up like a shell, my legs clasped in my arms. I take one of the novels from the stack and stare into its cover, and then I put the book on the floor of the closet. Slowly, I remove my cotton underwear and in the closet mirror I see my naked buttocks, muscles of submission. In my daydream, the lover has big white hands. He has no personality and isn't anyone I know in the visible world. He is a form, thick-thighed, like the British man on the book cover. He wears foreign khaki and I feel his trousers and the sharpness of his knee when I lie across his lap. I don't know if I am a piece of coal on fire, smoldering, or a flower, my flesh succulent like a petal.

I let the invisible world, with its invisible lover, bring me to enchantment; I let myself become a spirit and a star in those Jerusalem evenings, where outside, in the visible world, my mother and aunt are preparing to tell me what to wear for supper and what to do tomorrow when the day breaks, already deciding every detail of where I will go and how I will dress. I touch myself to feel the sensations again. *Here is Masada*, I think, and the hot desert, and streams of coarse things, like shrubs and cacti floating with the laundry, sheets and cloaks that the Bedouin wash, kneeling by the waters with their goats. I can explore it, my own body, climb like Masada, or maybe Hebron, with its strange sheikhs and warm soda water heated by the sun, and to which they add thick syrups of blackberry or raspberry or cherry, sweetening the fizz but still not stirring in any ice or cold water from the tap.

Feeling the tiny strip of pleasure now between my legs, I stir, like the syrups, all the sensations with my fingers. *It is my own mountaintop,* I think. *I am a nation.* In this motion, too, the long day, with my aunt and mother fighting and the bitterness that was inside my mother—foaming out like a belch that didn't care who else was in the room—all seem to disappear as I find my own body and its gifts, its soft skin. If it were a bird, it could fly out the window to the pine branch, to the dry shrubs and cacti in the distance, where the ice cream peddler is on the street.

Everywhere there is a sweet odor like the tulips outside the gate. I do not know why I like the fantasies, but it is my nation, this body, and the only power I will ever have. And then it feels like heaven, and a hot mist that circles from the screen and the glass mirror enters under the skin, where there might have been comfort or ecstasy, and I float with the hatboxes and the wooden leg hanging over me that replaces my uncle's amputated one, and with the blankets and the hats. What happens in my sex is built by my body for the final freeing of my selfhood from my mother.

*   *   *

It was in my early twenties, after my father suffered a tragic car accident and my relationship with my mother grew fractious, that I found this starting point again. Hospitalized for depression, I thought there were to be no more points at all, neither planes nor connections—no more existence. The present and past had been smashed; the future seemed only an endurance of fracture and dissolution. In the 1970s there were no medicines like Prozac or effective antidepressants.

The work I had to do toward health relied solely on bringing back fragments of identity and memory through a rigorous self-examination anchored in helplessness.

Sometimes, I believe my efforts to regain emotional stability had to run deeper than is necessary in our contemporary world we have now, one of drugs and accessible but revolving—eternally revolving—doors we call the mental health system. But I had learned long ago, during that summer in Jerusalem, how to visit closets and mirrors, how to come back to life though all of the senses. Therapy for despair was so much like feeling my flesh in that bedroom closet, my selfhood, a door closed to the overwhelming and ominous figures and places that disassembled me or threatened destruction or absorption so that no separate dignity of self was possible. I floated again in the sensations of my body and history—I unfolded myself, stretching through my trauma and loss, riding on shooting stars that would allow me back to that closet. Sometimes I took myself for a flame amid shadows. I allowed the black heart of my fantasies, sexual and hidden, to pulse again inside my body.

Had my sadness, my depression, really just been—as it was that summer in Israel, when I was eleven—a desire again for myself?

The morning of my discharge from Payne Whitney, I perused the form an aide brought in for me to sign. I suddenly wanted to draw beside my signature, and that of my attending psychiatrist, something, anything—a Jerusalem hill; a lavender sunset; streets and barren fields laid with barbed wire, yet still and forever borderless—that would connect the native land I hadn't known until then, that was now inside me. It had finally emerged, this time creating enough equilibrium for me to at least walk out of that hospital room and into the hope of a summer morning. On the form I was to sign was written:

WHITE FEMALE

AGE: 22

DIAGNOSIS: BORDERLINE PERSONALITY DISORDER

PROGNOSIS: GOOD

DATE RELEASED: JUNE 20, 1974

REASON GIVEN FOR DISCHARGE: NO LONGER A DANGER TO HERSELF

I signed the form and left the rest behind to a silence like the old secrets of the Kabbalah itself, or the spindly olive trees and dry bushes on the side of the Jerusalem roads, with the old Israeli army Jeeps and tanks that tourists see when they visit my mother's first land. In recovery from the severest parts of my mental illness, the door finally closed on the overwhelming and ominous figures and places inside that had deconstructed me, threatening destruction. I found the center, and it was potent and ineffable as the mysteries of my grandmother's land. In many ways, I would have to learn how to float in the enigmatic sensations of body and history with the others in my family.

How I Learned to Love My Body

Ellie McGrath

One summer, when I was two and a half, I went to visit my Aunt Mary and Uncle Jerry "for the weekend." I can remember getting out of their station wagon under the catalpa tree. They lived in Gloucester, Massachusetts, so I knew we would go to the beach, and I looked forward to playing with their Boston terrier, Torgie. I had no idea that I would not leave their home until I went away to college.

My mother had been diagnosed with breast cancer.

Back in the 1950s, "cancer" was a dirty word. No one said it aloud, except for doctors and nurses. Treatment options were very limited. There was surgery, of course, to remove the tumor, but no chemotherapy, only radiation. I have an old photo of my mother. It's summertime, we're outside, and my grandparents and I are smiling. My mother, painfully thin, is wrapped in a shawl. She has a faint smile, but her high cheekbones make her look cadaverous. I later learned she was not just thin; radiation had turned her skin green.

My mother would spend weeks in the hospital and sometimes come home, where she had round-the-clock nurses. But I remember most clearly the times she would stay in a nursing home. Whenever I visited her there, among the blind, deaf, and infirm, the old ladies would see me and try to touch me, a little girl in a Polly Flinders smocked dress. I'm sure I reminded them of their own children so many years earlier. One day, a woman with one arm reached out for me, saying, "Oh, come here, come here, I want to touch you." I had to stop myself from running away in terror.

Still, in some ways it was better for me when my mother was in the nursing home. At least I could visit her. When she was in the hospital, I would go outside her window and someone—probably my uncle—would hold me up so I could wave. Children were not allowed in hospitals. One Halloween, when I was six, I was dressed up as a little witch in a pointy hat and taken to Addison Gilbert Hospital. As we entered the lobby, I drew back. "No, I can't go in," I whispered to my aunt. "Children aren't allowed!"

"It's fine," my aunt reassured me. "We've talked to the doctors and nurses, and everyone thinks it would be nice for your mother to see you tonight." So in I marched, a little witch in black, carrying a pumpkin basket for treats.

Within a month, at the age of thirty-eight, my mother was dead.

I was frightened, bewildered, and inadequately consoled. The people around me said she had gone to heaven and would look over me. My father praised my mother as a fighter, a woman determined to "beat" the disease. "She was so smart," he'd add. "But she wasn't smart enough to go to a doctor when she first felt a lump." Maybe it was because she was raising a very young child, or perhaps she was exercising what today we call denial. "She'll always be young," my aunt would say wistfully. "Your mother will never have to grow old," as if that were a fate worse than death. One uncle, grasping for an explanation, sighed and said, "I guess some people are just unlucky."

I have another picture taken of me the year my mother died. I'm about to go to school, perhaps for the first day. My legs look like spindles. My clothes hang off me. I look as if a cocker spaniel could knock me over. I had pneumonia three times in a year. When I was taken to the beach for swimming lessons, the instructors said I was too weak to swim. As much as everyone tried to protect me and push me onward, I clearly absorbed my mother's death in a physical way.

I absorbed it mentally, too. From an early age, I understood how precarious life could be—pay attention or die. I was steeped in the lore of Gloucester fishermen drowning at sea, well before the movie *The Perfect Storm* was released. Terrible things happened all the time. I didn't care about how I *looked*; I cared about *surviving*. What scared me most was the threat from within: I saw my body as a potential enemy, one that could turn on me at any time.

I can't say exactly when I stopped living a worst-case-scenario life. Little by little, though, I became acquainted with my body. I learned to swim; I had so much natural buoyancy that I could float for hours. Despite being told I might have a heart attack if I rode my bike up a steep hill, I had no trouble doing so after the second or third time.

In college, I began riding long distances on my ten-speed racing bike. After graduating, I moved to New York City and got my dream job at *Time* magazine, back when women were hired as reporter-researchers. Within a few years, I became a writer for the magazine. I was suddenly turning into one of the lucky people.

As my self-confidence increased, I began to appreciate my body more. I began running, and within a year, I was one of the eighty-eight women in the first five-borough New York City Marathon. I trained myself to be powerful. I didn't just run 26.2 miles, I did so at a pace of less than seven minutes per mile. One Monday, I went in to work and an editor stuck his head into my office and said, "I saw you yesterday in that race in Central Park. I had no idea you were so fast." I could hardly believe that someone, a man, admired *me* as an athlete.

I began to confront my cancer phobia. At twenty-five, I had my first mammogram with a machine as big as a camera obscura. I dated a man I knew from running who was also an oncologist. He convinced me that there could be life after breast cancer. My running coach provided the proof: A year after her mastectomy, she passed me during the twenty-third mile of the Avon International Marathon in San Francisco. Not only had she beaten the cancer, she was running faster than I was! I continued to get annual mammograms. Once sonograms were available, I had one of those, too. I got married and—believing that I might actually survive—gave birth at the age of forty to my daughter. That was perhaps the luckiest moment of my life. Imagine! Forty years old, and able to get pregnant and give birth to what my obstetrician called a "perfect" baby girl. My body was performing feats I had never considered possible. I could imagine old age.

* * *

While I was pregnant, I was an editor at *Self* magazine. It was 1992 and I hired an assistant, Stephanie Williams, who was just out of college. Sharp and thin, a little nervous, but ambitious in a good way, Stephanie could understand dense medical journals and write snappy headlines with equal ease. She knew everything about popular culture that I didn't. When I told her I was pregnant, she kept my confidence until I was ready to make the announcement. After I gave birth, she was among the first to visit me at home. Even after we went on to different jobs, I helped guide her career; she pitched in when I had too much work.

I was on vacation in Maine in the summer of 2001 when I got an email from Stephanie with the header "Bad News."

"I hesitate to tell you this," she wrote, "because I know how upset you'll be. I can't believe that after all those years of watching you go to your mammograms and thinking, *Thank goodness that's not something I have to worry about,* I find myself with breast cancer."

Steph was right about my being upset. She had always had high blood pressure, which was odd since she was so thin. I used to encourage her to try running to bring it down. Her career was flourishing. She had just fallen in love with Daniel and believed he was The Man. Even though there had been no sign of a lump when she had seen her gynecologist a few months earlier, somehow the diagnosis was *late-stage* breast cancer. How could this have happened? She had just turned thirty, about the same age my mother had been when she was diagnosed. And, also like my mother, Stephanie had a lot to live for.

During the next year, she had twelve-hour surgeries to remove her breasts and reconstruct them, monthlong recuperations, chemotherapy, and radiation. Through it all, she remained upbeat and positive. After her final treatment in 2002, Stephanie and Daniel left for a romantic vacation in Italy. She was in Milan when she called her doctor to make sure that the last blood test was clean. The news was bad: Her tumor markers were up, which meant her cancer had metastasized. From that time on, Stephanie proceeded with fatalism. She knew she was going to die.

Everyone at some time imagines what they would do if they had only a year or a month or a day to live. That sense of time's winding down made Stephanie sit down at her laptop and begin writing the novel she had always wanted to write. It started out as a coming-of-age story about friends who had gone to the University of Pennsylvania, as she had. Trisha Portman, the protagonist, was not much like Stephanie. Trisha was a blond Pollyanna who worked in an art gallery and had dated the same man for years. Gradually, though, the novel began veering into Stephanie's new reality. She would eventually title it *Enter Sandman*, after Metallica's heavy-metal song about fear and comfort.

Before arriving at her Brooklyn apartment one day, I called to make sure she felt up for having a visitor. "I'm bald," she said, "and I don't want to wear my wig. It itches. Are you okay with that?" Was she testing me or warning me? I was determined not to blink. Still, it was shocking to see all that curly brown hair gone. Stephanie's eyes seemed bigger; her skin, whiter. I told her she looked like Sinéad O'Connor.

I never understood until I read the first draft of *Enter Sandman* how much Stephanie's hair meant to her. In the novel, Trisha, who has been diagnosed with breast cancer, talks to her best friend, Nat.

* * *

"I mean, really," Trisha said, "aren't my boobs and my life enough?" Actually, she had visions of overdosing before her hair started to go, but she didn't tell Nat this. "It's like, when I was being diagnosed, I was praying: Please, God, not the hair. Does that make me the vainest person on the planet? That I'd rather get my breasts cut off, throw up repeatedly, and die a slow, painful death than be bald?"

"No," Nat said. "It makes you a woman. . . . "

Every night, she awoke and tiptoed to the bathroom, where, under the fluorescent lights, she got her fix. At the sink, she shook her head vigorously (but not too vigorously), and counted the strawberry blond hairs that fell out. At first she'd find three, or nine or seven; then twelve, and then, finally, more than she could count.

After that, she stopped shaking her head, or even touching it, so as not to disturb the precious strands.

Now, when she tiptoed to the mirror in the middle of the night, she forced herself to look. She saw a genderless freak, or, worse, someone with cancer. She wanted to hurt herself, or lock herself in the bathroom and never come out, or force everybody in the world to shave their heads, too. To think that just the previous month, she had fretted over whether to have Andrea, her stylist, take off two inches or three.

Stephanie and I were driving to the Beekman Arms, an old inn in Rhinebeck, New York, one fall day. I thought lunch away from the city would be a nice treat. The leaves falling over the fieldstone walls and on the roofs of old mansions were golden with occasional bursts of red. Stephanie was talking about her book. "I hope I can finish it before I die," she said, "It doesn't bother you, does it, if I talk about my death?"

Well, yes, it did, but I couldn't really say so. Instead, I answered, "You don't know you're going to die. There may be a new drug that will work. You can't give up hope." She laughed. "I'm not giving up hope, but I get tired of people trying to act like it's not going to happen. Whenever I talk about dying to my doctor, she says, 'We're all going to die. I could be run over by a truck tomorrow.' I hate that. The chances she'll be run over by a truck tomorrow are practically zero, but it's pretty certain this disease will kill me."

*   *   *

When Stephanie finished the first draft of *Enter Sandman*, I urged her to take the book to an agent and find a publisher. Editors who read it told her that they thought the story had potential, but they didn't want Trisha to die. "No kidding," Stephanie and I would joke. I had been considering starting a small press. In early January 2004, Stephanie sent me the 125,000-word manuscript. I liked it, but another editor and I agreed it should be shorter. By February, the cancer had spread to Stephanie's lungs and she was back in the hospital. Her health was deteriorating rapidly. We talked about certain character changes and ideas about how to focus the narrative more, but I had my doubts about whether Stephanie was capable of doing the work. To my amazement, in early April, she sent me a stunning revision—shorter, more focused, a very good manuscript—and left the hospital. At this point, I realized that *Enter Sandman* simply had to live.

In early May, I incorporated a little publishing company as McWitty Press and sent the edited copy to the printer. The next day, Stephanie went back to Sloan-Kettering with a blood clot in her lung. I asked the printer to rush a preliminary galley to me, and on May seventh, I took it to Sloan-Kettering. Stephanie, who was barely conscious, looked at some pages, pulled off her oxygen mask, and said, "I thought the emails were going to be in a different typeface."

When the hospital finally managed to drain her lungs, I received an email from Stephanie saying, "Come over to the hospital, and we can start talking about the *Glamour* piece." She had nearly died, but she hadn't given up. Stephanie wrote a story, "Saying Goodbye to My Life," that ran in the September 2004 issue of *Glamour.* She wrote it to tell the world how much her life had meant to her and to generate interest in *Enter Sandman,* which she now saw as her legacy.

*   *   *

I've heard aging women say that the legs are the last to go. I don't think so. In Stephanie's case, it was her mind. On June tenth, I put the first bound copy of *Enter Sandman* in Stephanie's hands. The following Monday, we would have a book party for her at the Tea Lounge near her Park Slope apartment. Over the weekend, Stephanie realized that she had nothing to wear, *really* nothing to wear. She eventually settled on a silk madras skirt and matching wraparound blouse that belonged to my ten-year-old daughter. She wanted to look pretty, so she asked me to find a stylist who could do her makeup and hair, which had returned. Then, the night before the party, Stephanie's mood changed abruptly. She canceled the stylist. She had vowed that she would be carried to her book party like Frida Kahlo—aloft on a mattress—if necessary. But a couple of hours before the party, she said she couldn't go.

I was scared, afraid that she had kept herself alive just long enough to see the book become a reality. I had always heard stories of mothers hanging on until they see a child for the last time, and I worried that this party might be the end point for Steph. At six o'clock, however, she arrived on time, in good spirits, looking pretty and happy. An hour or so into the party, I made a short speech about how much I admired Stephanie, and how meaningful it had been to publish this book. And then, occasionally gasping for breath, Steph spoke eloquently about how much it had meant to have this book in her hands, how much it meant to her that so many of her friends were there. At one point, she said with a laugh, "This is almost like being at your own funeral. I feel like I've died and gone to heaven."

The next day, Stephanie stumbled over simple words. Then she lost her motor skills and had trouble walking. Four days later, her family took her back to the hospital for a brain scan, which indicated five tumors. When I visited her in the hospital, she may have sensed my presence, but she was beyond seeing me. On the third of July, at the age of thirty-three, Stephanie died.

*   *   *

Premenopausal breast cancer can spread like a prairie fire. In 1958, my mother's cancer metastasized to her spine and paralyzed her before it killed her. Nearly fifty years later— despite so many advances in diagnosis and treatment— Stephanie died of the same disease, the one she called the "queen bitch" of cancers. In the end, Stephanie hoped *Enter Sandman* would be a cautionary tale. "I want other women to realize that this can happen to *them*," she said. "Too many of us wait forever to start our lives."

In the hurry of every day, too many of us forget how precious life is. It can be way too short, as my mother and Stephanie learned. At fifty-four, I do Pilates to strengthen my core and yoga to stay flexible. I kayak, swim, and ski whenever I can. I take figure skating lessons and still work on my waltz jumps. I've obviously slowed down; I can barely run one mile at the pace I used to carry for twenty-six. But I still run several times a week, and friends joke that I'll be out there someday in Depends. In aging, you learn the art of compromise.

Every day, I thank my body for not betraying me. I can understand why women get plastic surgery or feel bad about their necks. I am not without vanity: I color my hair, which is blessedly thick, and wouldn't mind losing ten pounds. But I have an acute appreciation for the bottom line. It's a miracle to be able to get up every day, to be able to see the wrinkles, wiggle ten fingers, walk and talk, shiver and sneeze. Whenever I think of my mother and Stephanie, which is often, I thank my body for being my friend.

*   *   *

Enter Sandman (*McWitty Press*) *is available online at* *www.mcwittypress.com.*

Men Seldom Make Passes at
Girls Who Wear Glasses
Susanne Dunlap

In memory of my brother, Bruce, who was an eye doctor

When I came back to my house in Massachusetts, after a week of working at my day job in New York City, I tripped over a heavy package in the hallway.

"Been buying more books?" Charles said, in a gently accusatory tone. He was referring to a recent purchase I had made of what I thought would be five or six slim, half-calf volumes of a nineteenth-century costume reference, but that actually consisted of more than sixty pounds of hefty folio tomes that I could hardly lift.

Anyway, the box was not, as it happened, full of my latest guilty purchase. It was something I had completely forgotten about: My father had sent me a dozen or so photo albums my mother had assembled, chronicling her life before she met him.

I sighed, wondering where I would store these things in my overcrowded house. But as I lifted the albums out of the box, the temptation to open them and leaf through, just to satisfy my curiosity, overpowered me.

My mother died in 2000. My clearest memories of her focus largely on turbulent emotional times and a succession of illnesses. Yet these fraught memories combine with stories about her childhood that I used to love, and that were repeated at appropriate moments to impress or make some point. I had heard them so often that they felt more apocryphal than actual: the time she fell off the railroad bridge; the summers in Westhampton with Uncle Shrimp; the cottage on Lake Champlain and the boat whose anchor my mother had to swim down and free after it got stuck in a storm; quitting college because of a fight with her father; being an orderly at a mental hospital at age nineteen. The old photographs in the albums were strangely evocative, not of the mother I remembered, but of the stories she told. I could almost see my grandmother at our kitchen window, making Banbury tarts and telling me all the funny things my mother did when she was as young as I.

As I turned the pages of the albums, the mother I'd last seen dragging around an oxygen tank gradually distilled into a flesh-and-blood little girl, her adventures and misadventures caught by the camera, a girl with stories of her own; and, judging by the unfamiliar names and faces, there were many I had never heard, and would never have an opportunity to hear, except by deducing them from the fragments of her early life that had been captured on film. As a writer, I found the pictures, with their mute, suggestive narrative, utterly irresistible.

Abandoning all hope of being able to lay the albums aside and attend to other matters, I slipped into that absorbed state I have come to associate with the writing process, or rather, that part of writing that precedes actually putting any words on paper. I scrutinized the details of the photographs—the clothing, the expressions, the attitudes and poses—for clues about my mother's young life, about who she really was. Before long I began to fill in the spaces between each recorded moment, peering into the dark shadows of the images themselves, puzzling out the unwritten words between the notes in her neat, distinctive hand. Photoshop became my ally. I zoomed in on the scanned pictures, squeezing every ounce of detail I could out of them, getting frustrated that, too close up, they became blurry and pixelated, like the maps you find on the Internet.

After only a few hours, the pace at which I flipped through the pictures slowed. I found myself returning again and again to particular images. My mother as a bow-mouthed, sparkly-eyed toddler. Then as a five-year-old in a black and white summer garden, the sun dappling her with confidence, perhaps because she was aware of how cute she was with her '30s bob.

In the next album she was seven or eight, standing behind her little sister, five years younger and clearly my mother's pride and joy. At this point, I noticed an awkward gangliness that hadn't been there before. At first, I couldn't put my finger on what had changed since the earlier albums. It wasn't only that she had grown taller, and it wasn't the knobby knees hanging below her wide-pleated shorts. There was something else. And then I realized what was different: She was wearing glasses.

Of course, I knew my mother wore glasses. But I had never thought about her wearing glasses *as a child*. To anyone blessed with great eyesight, compared with traumas like serious illness and the loss of loved ones, the wearing—or not—of spectacles is laughably insignificant. But in that moment of realization, looking at her clear, pretty face behind the wire-rimmed glasses, I felt a deep connection with her. I could see, truly *see*, the instant in her life that was most like my own, an instant in which the world around me had changed for good.

From what I remember, I spent almost all of my early life separated from everything and everybody else by an object that made painful indentations on my nose and winged across my face. Life, starting at the moment when I got my first glasses, was viewable only through the magnification of a pair of carefully ground lenses.

I have just one actual memory of a time before glasses, although I have seen pictures of myself in that state. I was three. I sat halfway up the stairs to our apartment in Buffalo, in the precise location that would allow me to see myself reflected in the glass top of the Dutch door leading to the street. My mother used to dress me in dungarees with puffy-sleeved blouses underneath. From my special spot, I could imagine that the frilly blouse I wore was the top half of a beautiful gown, and that I was a princess—only my twirly skirt was hidden beneath the level of the reflecting glass. I spent hours talking to that image of myself, making up stories. The little girl who looked back at me did not wear glasses.

After that, the next image I see is of the noise-baffling tiles in the ceiling of my kindergarten classroom. I used to stare at them during rest period, until I made them get so close that they appeared only inches away. The effect fascinated me. I don't remember much else about kindergarten, but I remember missing a lot of school for a reason that annoyed and embarrassed me: My mother would come to take me to the eye clinic twice a week, or bring me in late, after I had had my appointment in the dingy downtown building. Yes, by that age I wore glasses. Half the time, my already annoying glasses were made more so by having one side patched to strengthen the other eye, or by having tape affixed to the edges of the lenses to force my eyes to look straight ahead. I had wandering eyes. They weren't crossed, but they weren't quite right. I spent an unbearable series of half hours doing eye exercises that made my eyes ache, following the technician's stick with one eye and then the other. How I hated that place. The torture of eye exercises continued all through elementary school, until the beginning of fourth grade, when the eye doctor finally realized they weren't accomplishing anything.

It was apparently my mother's genetic fault that three of her four children had weak eye muscles. I can see it in the pictures of her as a child, her eyes slightly off, as if she is looking not only at the camera but at something just over the photographer's shoulder. Perhaps that's why she paid such careful attention to our eyes. She didn't flinch at ensuring that we got corrective surgery. My younger brother and I went to the hospital together—it might have been a package deal, although I suspect it was just a way to concentrate into a shorter time span the aggravation of caring for a post-op child. I was nine and he was six. I would miss the first two weeks of fourth grade for this. But it didn't matter, everyone said. I was smart. I would catch up.

It's curious that I should have such a vivid image of this event—an event that, for a short time, deprived me of the ability to see at all—especially because so many other parts of my childhood have faded into nonexistence. I still have dreams about that hospital in downtown Buffalo. I remember the smell of the ether, counting backward, and then, after seemingly no time at all had passed, waking up and wanting to open my eyes and look around, reaching to feel the bandages and hearing my mother's voice telling me not to touch them. She brought me a rag doll from the hospital gift shop. I asked her to describe it to me. "It has yellow hair, and a pink gingham dress, and—"

"But what does yellow look like?" I asked. "What does pink look like?"

She answered by giving me examples of yellow things and pink things. But I couldn't *see* them, not even in my imagination. Colors had no meaning.

My eyes were covered for twenty-four hours, maybe a little more. I can still envision so clearly everything I saw the moment the doctor snipped away the bandages. The warm skin tones of his face and the bright point of light he waved in my eyes; the blue walls of the room; the yellow hair and pink dress of my new doll. The monochromatic image I had formed of my world was instantly bathed in color, as if someone had poured paint over everything. It hurt to move my eyes, but I did it anyway. The early fall sun lit the green leaves of the trees outside my window so that they glowed. I felt so grateful. The doll remained one of my favorites until I was too old for dolls.

So what about this other little girl, the one I've discovered in the photographs? When did she start to feel awkward in her glasses? Did she have the same emotions I did, a combination of relief and sorrow, every time I went to the optician's to pick out a new pair of spectacles? No one who is fortunate enough to have perfect eyesight can ever comprehend that feeling. I recall vividly the hope that I would find frames on the shelf that would make me look pretty. The frustrating exercise was compounded because I couldn't see what I looked like in the dummy frames without lenses in them. I'd have to get too close to the mirror to take in my whole face. And even if I could tell and thought I didn't look like a total freak, when my finished glasses came with their thick, distorting lenses, I usually cried. I cried, that is, until I went outside and looked up and could see the leaves in the trees. The world was clear. And that came at a price.

In grade school, who you were was cruelly determined by how your friends saw you. When they looked at me, my friends saw a nerd with glasses. Popularity did not attach to such people. None of the fairy princesses in the storybooks wore glasses. None of the contestants in the Miss America pageant wore glasses. The fact that my mother, father, and all my brothers wore glasses made not the slightest difference. I don't even remember if any of my friends wore glasses. Glasses were my particular cross to bear, my red letter, my brand. "You know Susie Dunlap; she has glasses and long hair."

I used to fantasize about a handsome prince's falling in love with me despite my glasses, gently lifting them off my nose and gazing into my blue eyes (the dents from the glasses would have magically disappeared), telling me he'd never seen a more beautiful girl. Then he'd ask me to marry him (because, let's face it, even in the early '60s, we were still bred to believe that a girl's future lay in the arms of a man who would take care of her forever).

But what of my own mother? After the age of eleven or so, the pictures of her start to vacillate between glasses and no glasses. Candid pictures, where she hasn't had time to remove them, show her with those 1940s pointy frames (a style that lasted through the '50s and into the '60s). It's hard to see her eyes behind them. In posed pictures, she is a willowy, elegant girl who looks much older than fifteen or sixteen, with her high cheekbones and Lauren Bacall eyes. There's only one picture where she's looking directly at the camera with her glasses on. She looks so happy. The picture was taken by a man who was not my father. That photographer also took pictures of her without her specs. In those she looks lost, a little blind, absent. That's the funny thing about nearsighted people: You can usually tell, even when they don't wear glasses. My mother never wore contact lenses, even when she could have traded in her glasses for them. As far as I remember, she never expressed to me any discomfort or self-consciousness about wearing glasses, at least not as an adult. Ironically, it was my mother who first quoted Dorothy Parker to me: "Men seldom make passes at girls who wear glasses," even before I knew what it meant to make a pass. But she always followed it with a quote from one of her literary heroes, Ogden Nash:

> A girl who is bespectacled
> She may not get her nectackled
> But safety pins and bassinets
> Await the girl who fassinets.

(I never quite understood how wearing glasses failed to protect my mother from the safety pins and bassinets.)

Self-confident mother or no, at the age of fifteen I got contact lenses. I think I can safely say my world changed the moment I no longer had to see it through a wall of clear plastic. But I'm not altogether certain it changed for the better. Suddenly, I wasn't that brainy Dunlap girl who played the piano, a little awkward but nice enough. I was the girl with the most coveted boyfriend, the girl who turned heads everywhere she went, for whom men offered to buy drinks even when she was out with her mother. It took a while for this girl to be quite comfortable with the power she had over men—power that seemed entirely dependent on not wearing glasses, despite the fact that many other things about her had changed as well.

I think it was then that I discovered something important about my eyes: It wasn't about being able to see; it was about being seen. Throughout my varied adult life, no matter what I've done, feeling attractive has always been just as important as achieving.

Around the time my mother died, I started having to wear reading glasses. At first I did so over my contact lenses, but my bad eyesight deteriorated pretty quickly, and it wasn't long before I needed two pairs of reading glasses: one for reading, one for working at the computer. I decided then that my eyes had finally defeated me. I had come full circle. Why struggle with contact lenses and two pairs of reading glasses when I could have progressive lenses and be able to look up from a book or the computer screen and actually see across the room?

I believe it's no coincidence that only in these last five years, after returning to wearing glasses all the time, have I become a serious writer. In a curious fashion, the annoying accessory that prevented me from seeing myself as attractive now reflects me back into my own mind. I've drawn my spectacles like a curtain across the rest of the world, hiding behind them and kidding myself that people can't really see me. The dreamy, withdrawn child has become the introspective, reclusive adult who is happiest typing on her laptop or reading a book. The three-year-old looking into the top half of the Dutch door has crawled back into my heart and taken up residence there.

It was fun while it lasted, beauty. But I have come to accept that the elegant, cosmopolitan woman with the contact lenses wasn't really me. No matter what I have done to disguise it or correct it, my bad eyesight has defined who I am more than any other physical attribute. Everything about my world is informed, literally, by the way I see it.

So, as I lovingly sort through the photographs of my mother, I push my glasses up my nose every now and again to bring the images into sharper focus. I'll never know how the girl in the pictures truly felt about wearing glasses, but that doesn't matter. What matters is that I can finally put my own experience into perspective. It's all clear to me now—as clear as it can be, that is, to someone whose naked eyes have never truly seen the world as anything but a colorful blur.

Belly Wounds

Caroline Leavitt

I always believed in self-improvement.

At seventeen, I had my hook nose bobbed. In my thirties, I colored away all my gray. I always did the sit-ups I loathe, just so my belly could hold its own in a skintight dress. I scrupulously covered what I couldn't correct—makeup over dark circles, long sleeves over ungainly arms, long pants or skirts over bowed legs. I had all my beauty bases covered.

And then, ten years ago, three days after giving birth, I became critically ill from a rare blood disease, and for more than a year, my whole appearance changed in a way I could do nothing about, a way I can describe only as horrifying. My hair fell out in clumps. My skin turned gray. Steroids puffed me from swizzle-straw thinness to near obesity.

Five emergency operations gave my belly a weird new geography; it formed a hard triangle on one side and cleaved down the center, and my belly button moved far to the right.

It took me more than a year to get back to normal—or as normal as I'm going to get. I'm thin again, my hair is back, my skin is rosy. Only my belly remains, still so misshapen I've given up form-fitting clothes, still so large that sometimes on the subway, people smile and ask pleasantly, "What do you want, a boy or a girl?" The doctors tell me I can have a tuck done and fix this last vestige of my illness. But I, Ms. Physical Insecurity, the onetime queen of self-improvement, now choose, deliberately, defiantly, to keep it.

Before I got sick, I had a lot of ideas about what body "perfection" meant. I wasn't going to let myself go as a new mother. I was going to exercise myself back into my form-fitting clothes, keep my hair long, wear makeup.

But the reality was different.

Sick, I could hardly get out of bed, and my odd new shape meant that I certainly couldn't fit into any sexy dresses. "Oh, that's the meds," my hematologist told me. "But it goes away eventually."

Eventually, I told myself. But I kept increasing, going up one size, and then two. My eyes began disappearing into pin dots in my fleshy face. My chin doubled and then moved into triplicate. And then, as I bent over my son to tickle him, a long, thick fistful of hair slid down my shoulder and onto my baby, and I burst into terrified tears.

In a desperate act of self-preservation, I began to avoid mirrors, to hide in the house. When people called, wanting to visit, I feigned exhaustion. When people dropped by, I pretended to be asleep, the covers over my head. The only places I would go were doctors' offices thrice weekly and a friend's deserted house in the country, and even then I stayed inside.

Jeff, my husband, put his arms around me. "You know I think you're beautiful," he said quietly.

"That's just because you love me," I said hopelessly. He sighed, shaking his head.

I probably would have stayed inside for the duration of my illness, but our bills began to pile up. Our insurance company began balking, refusing payments, and disability refused to cover my staying home any longer. Jeff's job as a freelance writer wouldn't begin to cover our mounting expenses. To my horror, I had to go back to work; even worse, it was in style-conscious Manhattan.

When I was well, I used to go to work in form-following suits, in tight '50s sweaters and little skirts. I wore my hair in a long riot of waves. I accentuated my pale skin with only a little red lipstick and a lot of black mascara.

I called some of my coworkers to prepare them for my altered appearance, to make it easier for myself. "Listen, I look really different," I stammered. "Really terrible." People laughed. "Come on. We can't wait to see you!"

I bought a new dress for my first day back at work. It billowed to my ankles, a size large where I usually took a small. My hair was gray, too fragile, too sparse, to color, and the few strands I had left, I had tucked into a small tail in back. I put on some blush, some lipstick, some mascara. *I can do this,* I told myself.

On the subway, two thin women in black Lycra looked at me and whispered to each other. A little girl stared frankly.

And a man, a concerned look on his face, stood up and helped me into his seat. When I got to my office, everyone seemed to be crowded around my desk. They blinked at me. "You look great!" one woman blurted overenthusiastically. People hugged me, they had presents, but I saw how every once in a while someone averted her eyes, a tiny gesture that struck me like a slap.

My favorite story—now, not then—is about the time I had to pick up a freelance writing job at another company, known for its line of sexy lingerie. I had worked for the account executive before, a thin, stylish woman with a waterfall of blond hair, who told me she had months of work for me.

"Don't warn her about your looks," Jeff pleaded. "You have to give people a chance. And anyway, it's her problem if she reacts, not yours." So I didn't tell the woman about my changed appearance, but when I walked into her office, she flinched and then quickly composed herself. She was perfectly pleasant, but she never gave me work again.

Daily, I lost more and more hair. I kept swelling. I called wig places. I begged my doctors to make me look normal again. "Hair grows back," the doctor told me. "Your belly can be surgically fixed. But not until you're off your meds and well."

"When am I going to look normal?" I cried to my husband. "Everyone is looking at me."

"Screw them," Jeff said. "You're alive. The baby and I love you. Who cares?" He began gathering things from around the house. "Come on," he said. "We're all going out."

"I can't go out looking like this."

But he shook his head, adamant. "We're going," he insisted.

It was a beautiful spring day and we went into the city. We pushed the baby in the stroller, and after a while I was having too good a time to notice whether anyone was staring. I felt happy.

"What did I tell you?" Jeff said.

It still wasn't easy for me, but I felt as if I had turned a corner. I began venturing out more and more, and each time felt as if I were immunizing myself against shame. And then, a week later, when I was carefully arranging what hair I had left, I felt something poking through. A new silky tuft. I stared delightedly at myself in the mirror, and I suddenly noticed the contours of my face again. A peach tone in my gray skin.

One sweltering day when we were out, when I was in my usual long sleeves and long pants, I suddenly couldn't stand how hot I felt. I knew I still looked terrible, so what did it matter if I looked even more terrible, if I bared my bowed legs, my gangly arms? Looking genuinely off-kilter made all my imagined body slights seem, well, ridiculous and petty.

I veered into a store and bought a sleeveless minidress. I walked out wearing the dress, ridiculously triumphant, as if I had scaled a great height. "Look at you!" Jeff said, slinging an arm around my shoulders. All that summer I wore that dress. It was cool, comfortable, maybe even symbolic. Every time I even touched it, I felt good.

In all, it took me about a year to recover. My hair, thicker and glossier, shot down to my shoulders again. My skin turned luminous. Only my belly, disfigured, puffed out as if pregnant, remained. "You can get that fixed now if you want," the doctors told me. It was what I had been waiting to hear, what had kept me going for nearly a year, and now I realized, to my great surprise, that I no longer wanted to. It no longer seemed to matter.

It has now been more than ten years since I got sick. I look normal. People don't stare at me anymore, except the occasional man wanting to flirt. Even my belly has gone down enough that the only thing someone might think is, *Boy, she needs to do sit-ups.*

And I have come to love my belly. For me, my belly is almost a badge of honor, my very own purple heart, proving I've been through the wars and come out victorious, reminding me how silly worrying about blotchy skin or graceless arms is in the face of having something really wrong with your body.

It's a reminder to me, too, about what appearance really is—not something to be taken too seriously. "Who cares?" my husband said, and he was and is right. Love my belly, love me. I've come to love both. And I keep the big-shirt companies in business.

This essay first appeared on Salon.com, March 23, 2000.

The Puzzle of My Body

Susan Ito

Half and Half

I was adopted when I was three months old by parents who loved me but who looked quite different; we were carved from unalike trees. Where their skin was caramel brown, mine was freckly and pinkish, even more so after being in the sun. They were Japanese and I was, too, but not completely. I was what they called *hambun-hambun*, or half and half. Now I call myself *hapa*, or part Asian. I had been born, they told me, to a woman who was Japanese American, like them. But my other half was a blank, a mystery. Something strong-gened, whose Caucasian features threatened to smother my Asian ones.

I could see, from living with them and close to my extended family, what made me different from them: I was hairy, much hairier than they were. Once I hit adolescence, I was horrified to sprout hair on my knuckles, on the top of my toes, and in a furry blanket over my arms and legs. I had an impressive unibrow. I spent hours bent over the bathtub with razors, tubes of stinking Nair, and bleach that made my eyes sting. My parents knew nothing of being overly hirsute; they had only the gleaming black hair on their heads. Their bodies were smooth as chestnut wood.

My hair was thick, coffee brown, and riddled with unruly bumps and waves: cowlicks and twists and turns that I couldn't control. I longed for the "real" Japanese hair that my cousins had: inky black and straight.

My parents were short. I was taller than both, although not tall. Neither of them wore glasses until they were well into their seventies; I received my first heavy-duty prescription when I was seven. With 20/600 vision, I am legally blind. When I was old enough to wear contacts, I leaped at the chance and wore them for years.

What Are You?

You must be Italian, some people said. No. Puerto Rican. Hawaiian? Jewish. *You no Japanese!* (So said the Chinese woman at the dry cleaner.) I think you look more Korean than Japanese. Are you part Indian? What are you? What's your other half?

Half of the Mirror

When I was twenty years old, I searched for my birth mother. I found her one wintry March day in a hotel room in the Midwest. She opened the door to my knocking, and I was stunned to see a woman who was exactly my height. Her lips were identical to mine and so was her round-cheeked face. I stared. She stared back.

During the next several hours, as we told each other stories of the decades that had passed, I looked at her surreptitiously. I did a silent inventory of our bodies. We both wore contact lenses: She had the same atrocious myopia as I did.

I attributed the ways in which we were different to the genes of my invisible, unnamed birth father. Obviously, he was the one who had contributed the hairy knuckles and toes. The freckles. He was the one who had put the slight wave in my hair and tinted it darkish brown rather than black.

I snuck a look at her chest. Her breasts were small, neat, what I referred to longingly as "teacup breasts." My own chest, popping the buttons on my blouses, must have come from *his* mother, his grandmother, his aunts.

Who is he? I asked. *What* is he? She wouldn't say.

Our Legs

One weekend, she came to New York for business. She was staying at the Plaza Hotel overlooking Central Park. Would I like to come from New Jersey for an overnight visit?

I was dazzled. She wore her hair in a perfect Cleopatra haircut and was dressed in a crisp red and black suit and unusual, artistic jewelry, like something from an art museum's gift shop. Had I really come from her? I felt awkward and ugly-ducklingish in my college jeans and clogs, my puffy down coat.

She said she'd shower before we went for dinner. And in that moment when she stepped out of that steamy little room wearing no more than a thick white towel, I knew we were related. I stared with huge eyes at her legs, at my legs, the first time I'd seen them on another human being. Muscular, with sturdy thighs and that particular curve of the calf. Her ankles were my ankles. Our identical patellae nodded at each other.

My legs were truly my only source of corporal pride. I had complaints about pretty much every other aspect of my body: My hands were too big; my skin, too hairy; my ears, too crooked; my hair, not black or straight enough. But my legs, I had always been proud of them. People often said, "You must be a swimmer/runner/gymnast," when in fact I was as unathletic as they come. My legs were unearned prizes, and they made me glad.

It was then, when I saw her in that towel, that I knew, *really* knew, she was my mother. I thanked her for the legs, and she laughed and pulled on her pants, and we went for a walk through Central Park.

In the middle of the night, I suddenly awoke, realizing that my mother was sleeping four feet away. It was the first time we had ever passed a night together. I gave myself over to the pleasure of staring at her face, slowly examining her eyebrows. I memorized the curve of her nose, how it was much flatter than my own. I stared at her small square hands, at her perfectly straight, perfectly black hair. She slept unaware, turning her naked face toward me, and I took it in with a hunger that overwhelmed me.

Frisbees

I moved to San Francisco and she visited a few times. She was a vendor of promotional items, specializing in Frisbees, and one of her assignments was covering the Ultimate Frisbee Olympics in Golden Gate Park. She introduced me to one of the Frisbee champs, a man named Matt. He was tall, flexible as a rubber band, and appealingly sweaty. He bounced lightly on his heels as he shook my hand and said with a nod, "Nice to meet you." Then he turned to her, winked, and said, "She's very pretty. Like mother, like daughter."

He'd said it: Those words, the Pandora's box, Rumpelstiltskin-break-the-spell-damned-to-hell-forever words. I stared with my mouth open, waiting for him to fall down dead on the spot. Then it occurred to me that maybe it wasn't a mistake, that maybe she'd told him, maybe he knew exactly who I was, maybe it was obvious, and we were all standing there on that sunny afternoon with the truth shining for everyone to see. I snapped my head in her direction, grinning like a golden retriever. Then I saw that something in her face had changed radically: She was still smiling, her dimple was showing, but the light behind her eyes had been pinched out. In a voice that was chipper, gay, a note or two higher than usual, she said, "Matt, my daughter

is back in Minneapolis. This is *Susan,* a friend of the family."
She emphasized the word "friend," and let "family" drop
into less than a whisper.

Matt raised his eyebrows. "Well. Whatever. All you
Orientals look alike; what can I say?" He ducked as she
shrieked and swatted at him with a Frisbee, and the moment
was broken.

Girdle

When I asked her how it was possible to go seven months
into pregnancy without anyone's knowing, she looked away.
"I didn't eat much," she said. "I wore tight clothes so it was
hard to tell. And a girdle."

When she told me this, I was twenty years old and I'd
never been pregnant. The idea seemed reasonable enough at
the time: Something's too big, you squeeze it down to size.
I'd seen it work, like a six-foot sleeping bag compressed into
a nylon bag the size of a bread loaf.

But eventually I married and became pregnant with
my first child, and I was shocked at how round and
tense my belly grew. The baby punched its foot against
my palm, the knobby outline visible through my T-shirt.
I thought about that girdle, and it felt as if the oxygen
were being squeezed from my chest. I played hide-and-
seek with the baby, from one side of my abdomen to the
other: Poke, I found it with my thumb; poke, it kicked
me back. Sometimes it tickled, and sometimes it felt like
an attack.

I see her in her running shorts, I remember that moment when I first saw those legs on another person, in that hotel room in New York City. These are good legs.

Growing Older

My body, as it ages, is resilient and weak in the same places as hers. Like her, I have astronomically high blood pressure. I exercise regularly to keep it at a good level, and every morning I swallow three colored pills. She takes slightly different pills, but they do the same thing. We have the shadow of her own mother hanging over us, the grandmother who never knew I existed, who died of an instant stroke when she was fifty. "Too much soy sauce," my birth mother says. "High blood pressure, and she didn't take care of it."

I met her recently at a San Francisco bistro, and I am awed by how youthful and beautiful she still looks, now into her seventh decade. I feel a flutter of pride and hope that she has passed these good-aging genes on to me.

But time has made me weary of trying, year after year, to solve the puzzle of my body, to untangle the question of my other invisible heritage.

She still has her beautiful dimples, her dazzling smile. She still, after all this time, has impressive legs. She still holds the key to the riddle, my lifelong question: Who and what was he? And what am I?

Dead Bone

Aimee Liu

Every evening at eight o'clock, a middle-aged woman who reminds me of myself hobbles past my house. She wears black leggings and reflective sweats, her hair drawn into a ponytail that jerks sideways as she hurls herself forward. This mystery woman leaves her car down the block, while putting mileage on her body instead.

When I first moved to this low-traffic neighborhood six years ago, she jogged up the brightly lit center of the road with brisk, purposeful strides. Then she began to favor one ankle and gravitated toward the curb. Elbows sharp, hips swiveling, she switched to racewalking. Through time, her form progressively deteriorated, but she never missed a single night. Now she contorts her knees and torso, her gait crablike and her pace just ahead of a crawl. The only thing about this woman that doesn't match my past self is her preternaturally blond hair.

Though I'm often in front of my house when my alter ego passes, she does not look up—at me or at anyone. Her face and posture make it clear that she is as intent on her bodily pain as the most devout self-flagellant. Yet if I were to demand why she chooses to subject herself to such punishment, I doubt religion would be her explanation. Instead, from behind the same mask of defensive superiority that I used to wear, she would tell me she does it for her health.

Fitness, beauty, energy, health—how well I know those self-righteous excuses. For the sake of my "looks," I dropped thirty pounds at the start of adolescence and held my weight below one hundred (the picture that comes to mind now is that of a child holding a terrified cat underwater) until my last year of college. In the name of "nutrition," I refused to eat meat from age fourteen to thirty-five, when my consequent lethargy finally bordered on blackout. To "shape up" as a teenager, I would go for four-hour bike rides, during which I refused to downshift even when climbing forty-degree hills. Pain, to my thinking, meant gain. The more my body hurt, the more my willpower gloated. A war was under way, my physical constitution its battleground. Health was no more my real goal than cheap tea was the object of the American Revolution. The celebrants at the Boston Tea Party, however, enjoyed one advantage over masochists like the eight o'clock jogger and me: They understood that they were fighting a war of independence.

We exercise zealots instead believed that ours was a higher cause. The logic that guided us was the same that has, through the centuries, justified foot binding, corsets, plastic surgery, and hair shirts—a logic that equates perfection with unnatural suffering. Far from fighting an oppressive king, we voluntarily reduced and mortified ourselves in the name of the current king of culture: fitness. Maybe, we thought, if we ran just a few more miles a day, or worked off another hundred calories on the StairMaster, or spent another half hour at the gym, we'd finally stop worrying about not looking or acting or being good enough. Then, at last, we'd feel free—without having to rebel against anyone except our physical selves.

*   *   *

My personal assaults on my body date way back. As a child, I had so little sense of my dimensions or boundaries that I regularly walked into walls. The resulting bruises surprised and fascinated me, since I rarely recalled the particular collisions that had caused them. I unconsciously scratched mosquito bites until they bled. I peeled off scabs and more than once stripped my thumb of its nail all the way to the cuticle. I hated being alone with my body, which may have been either cause or effect of the solitude that dominated my childhood. My only sibling was eight years older. My father, a commuting executive, spent his days and many evenings in the city. My mother was preoccupied with her import business. No other children lived in our wooded Connecticut estate-turned-private-enclave, and in my classmates' more typical suburban neighborhoods, with their tract houses, sidewalks, and resident cliques, I felt like a trespasser.

My parents, understandably, denied my pleas to move to one of those "normal" neighborhoods. They loved the quiet and grace of our home, which they'd built, largely with their own hands, before I was born. In time, I would see their point. What they could not understand, however, and what I see clearly only now, is that I was so uncomfortable in my skin that it hardly mattered where I lived, or, for a long time, with whom.

My heart, that covert stage director, dramatized some of my self-warfare to appear accidental. When I whipped out a mat knife at the 1973 open-air Summer Jam in Watkins Glen, my nineteen-year-old impulsiveness seemed a reaction to the ninety-degree heat. My boyfriend (my first) urged caution as I dug into the jeans I was wearing. I meant to convert them to cutoffs. At the sound of his voice, however, the blade flew off course, slitting my lower calf. The suddenly revealed layers of skin looked like parting lips. Blood coursed down my leg as Country Joe & the Fish sang over our heads, "Whoopee! We're all gonna die." My boyfriend wrapped Kleenex around the wound as I continued to slash at the remaining fabric, intent on completing my task. He came home with me that night and stayed for a week to tend to my injury. Two months later, he threw a glassful of wine in my face when I told him I didn't love him. I didn't dare love anyone.

Running a finger over the thirty-year-old scar, I can still feel the indentation where the blade cut through muscle, nearly to bone. The wound should have been stitched. My first boyfriend and I, however, were well matched in our habit of urging each other through physical feats, such as walking backcountry roads all night, or fasting for a week, or restricting our fluid intake to strong black coffee. Privation was an essential component of our relationship: Stitches did not occur to either of us.

My senior year in college—after learning that my second boyfriend was still seeing the ex-wife from whom I'd thought he was divorced—I became bulimic. Overdosing on hoarded cookies and cake, and then getting rid of them, I acted out each night what he'd taught me about love. My body bore the brunt. My distraction was complete. One morning I missed the step outside my dorm room, ripping the tendons in my right ankle so badly, I could hear them snap. Though I couldn't walk, I refused to consult a doctor and didn't know to ice the joint. Tanqueray served as my anesthetic.

After graduating, I moved to Manhattan and took as a lover a man I knew I didn't love. His primary girlfriend, a model absurdly named Boo, was working in Paris that summer. Come fall, he informed me that Boo was returning and I needed to remove my belongings from his Upper East Side apartment. A few nights later I tripped over a rolled kitchen mat at the end of my waitressing shift. The tray of glass vases I was carrying fell to the floor. My right palm came down on a broken rim, followed by my full weight. I stood. Before I went into shock, I marveled at the anatomical depth, the universe of circuitry, exposed inside my hand. My lover waited with me for a surgeon at New York Hospital until 3:00 AM. Together, we watched the orderlies wheel in a geriatric couple spattered with blood. The orderlies debated fruitlessly whether the old folks' attempt to kill each other was meant to be suicide or homicide. After four hours of surgery, I was promised motion but no sensation in the

three affected fingers. Eventually I would file a worker's
compensation claim. My lover, who owned the restaurant
where I'd worked, was legally liable for the kitchen staff's
failure to erect a HAZARD sign over the mat that they furled
while mopping the floor. But I knew Brown, the cook, and
Fong, the busboy. It wasn't their fault. It was no one's fault.
Accidents just happen.

Today, a crescent-shaped scar runs from just below my
right lifeline to the inside of my wrist. The surgeon told me
I was lucky the glass didn't (quite) sever my radial artery.
After thirty years, the tips of my right thumb, forefinger,
and middle finger remain senseless. This makes touch-typing
impossible, buttons and necklace clasps formidable. I make
love with one hand.

* * *

When I see the mystery woman hobbling past my house,
I am tempted to hug her and shake her, but I know she
would only pull away from me, another know-it-all stranger.
To resound, the message would have to come from a much
closer source, from that very body she insists on abusing for
reasons she cannot fathom. Only when this instrument of
distraction betrays her by declaring its own independence
will she be forced to separate metaphor from the deeper
hungers that drive her.

All the accidents of my youth failed to warn me off running.
To my detriment, I entered adulthood in the era of Jim Fixx
and the fitness revolution. Fixx lived in my hometown and

wrote in *The Complete Book of Running* about many of the same bucolic courses I had enjoyed walking as a child. He replaced smoking with running at thirty-five, dropped fifty pounds, and began writing books that extolled the medical, spiritual, and psychological benefits of self-propulsion. Fixx sparked the national boom of 5Ks, 10Ks, marathons, triathlons, and ultramarathons that persists to this day. Though never fluid or easy on my feet, I became a convert. Jogging five or more miles a day was guaranteed to cure what ailed me. When Fixx dropped dead of a heart attack while out on one of his daily runs at age fifty-two, I chose to ignore the news.

My husband was an eight-mile-a-day runner when we met. He was also fourteen years older, an accomplished film producer with a young son. I pushed myself to prove that I could keep up with him—and that I was fitter than his two previous wives—even though I had no money and no job and had left my friends and family three thousand miles away to join this man in Los Angeles. My husband ran because he liked to run and because he was a natural, steady and easy on his feet. He ran because it helped his basketball game. He ran because it was something we could do together. Whenever he angered or upset me, instead of fighting or working the problem out *with* him, I'd run away, covering marathon distances solo.

Endorphins, nature's opiates, kicked in reliably around mile three, mimicking euphoria and masking my damaged ankle's complaints. Just as I had when surviving on eight hundred calories a day, I prided myself on my discipline and endurance. Suffering remained my path to perfection. One day at work I mentioned my new long-distance passion and an astute colleague replied, "I'm sorry." I feigned bemusement but didn't stick around for her to explain what I should by then have known: Sooner or later, I'd run into a wall.

My body finally quit without warning—or, more accurately, after thirty-five years of warnings—one day in 1989, as I sat watching my three-year-old son dance around the family room. I glanced down and noticed that my ankle had swollen to the size of a grenade. When I tried to stand, the joint felt as if it had been detonated. Several rounds of x-rays and MRIs ensued. The diagnosis: avascular necrosis. Translated literally, this means "without blood, death." In my case, it meant that the blood supply to my bone had been severed. As a result, bone tissue was dying. The bone in question was the talus, central to my right ankle. "No precipitating event," the orthopedist jotted on my chart. My body, like a long-suffering wife, was reacting not to any specific assault but to years of abuse.

Left alone, the bone would continue to deteriorate. Drugs offered no solution; ankle joint replacements in 1989 had a worse-than-dismal success rate. The only option that held any real hope was experimental: Living bone could be scooped from my pelvis and grafted onto the talus to replace the dead bone. Recuperation and regeneration should take about six months. If the procedure succeeded, the surgeon would write it up for a journal article, trumpeting a new scientific breakthrough. "What choice do we have?" my husband asked rhetorically.

The videotape that documents the procedure shows gravel being packed like dental filling inside a cavity. Streamers of debris rush past the lens into the surgeon's vacuum. Once the cavity is full, the surface is polished smooth. The video could be a primer on internal housekeeping.

"Be patient," my doctor said, when I asked how soon I could expect to be up and about. "Bone grows slowly. Give it time."

Patience had never been my virtue. Now it took me by force. We hired an able-bodied au pair to take my son to preschool and play with him after school at the park. My husband managed our nine-year-old's days, leaving me to spend mine on my back with my ankle cast above my head. I studied the cymbidium beside my bed as it slowly came into bloom. On an old drawing pad, I sketched the play of white blossoms like the opening and closing patterns of a ballet. Each flower's course was implicit, its perfection unmistakable, yet what did it suffer to achieve such beauty? If I pried one of those long pregnant buds open too soon, or forced it to overcome obstacles—a band holding it closed, say, or deprivation of water and light—the result, at best, would be distortion. More likely, the bud would simply wither and die without blooming at all.

I daydreamed about the child we hoped to have after I recuperated. Perhaps it would be a girl. After a bit more reflection, I thought I would teach her to follow my husband's and sons' examples instead of my own. Our three-year-old son danced and sang. His first word was "ball," and, like his father, he loved the touch, the roll, the feel of, and the chase after, round playful objects. My stepson preferred construction. He could spend days on his knees, transforming the family room into a Lego space station. He and his father together built rockets that actually launched, flashing skyward at hundreds of miles per hour before springing their miniature parachutes and drifting back to earth. My boys knew what they loved and why. These pursuits made my sons feel good because they were fun, and because they could be shared with others, which was how the boys made friends. They could no more imagine denying themselves these sources of love than they could deny their need for love itself. Neither, I vowed, would my daughter. And neither, from now on, would I. My body had finally, definitively, forced the message over my perverse will: I could no longer afford the fallacy that pain would make me better.

*   *   *

First crutches, then canes, then braces, Ace bandages, and orthotics replaced my running gear. For the next two years I limped after my exuberant preschooler, watched my husband shoot baskets with the boys in the back yard, and sat on the sidelines at my stepson's soccer games as the rest of the parents stood and cheered. My ankle did not cooperate as planned. My surgeon's hopes for that journal article faded, along with mine for another child. My body was now calling the shots, each painful step rebuking me for pushing it too far.

Patience forced me to remember how I loved to walk. I loved the leisure of it, the freedom and ease, the looking, breathing, and listening that seemed as natural and intrinsic to perambulation as the roll from heel to toe. When I was a child out for a stroll in Connecticut, one of the reasons I would collide with walls was that I was preoccupied by the patterns sunlight made on the canopy of leaves overhead. Later, freed from suburbia to Manhattan as a teenager, I would saunter up Park Avenue, hunting the nineteenth-century busts and gargoyles and art deco flourishes that hid under the rooflines of skyscrapers. Throughout one summer in Europe, I would rise at six to explore the farmers markets and memorize the streets of Vienna, Paris, Rome. As a new Los Angeles transplant, I'd take my young stepson to the beach, and as we walked the tide line we'd remark how the surf made it seem like the ocean was breathing, how the sand yielded differently beneath our feet if we curled or stretched our toes. In Venice during Carnevale, my husband and I donned feathered masks and roamed from piazza to piazza, celebrating each unpredictable turn, enjoying our shared abandon.

I loved those walks for precisely the opposite reason that I starved or ran or fought my body: They made me feel connected. To the land, to cities, to nature—to the light, life, and people I loved. Those walks didn't hurt. They were no penance in the name of "health." They didn't make me feel superior, but they made me feel good and genuinely happy. And when I had my family with me, I could share that happiness. Of course, I have no proof, but I do not believe that those walks disconnected the blood from my bone. I suspect they had exactly the opposite effect.

*   *   *

What matters most after any war are the terms of truce. Eleanor Roosevelt wrote, "It isn't enough to talk about peace. One must believe in it. And it isn't enough to believe in it. One must work at it." Today, I work at keeping the peace with my body by honoring its needs instead of denying them. When hungry, I eat until satisfied. When tired, I sleep. When anxious, I sit quietly, meditating on water or sky or the play of sunshine on the foliage in my back yard. As for exercise, I move as I can, for pleasure, not for pain. I love to swim, but I don't count laps or set the kind of rigid distance requirements I would have in my meaner days. I love to ride bicycles with my family at the beach, now respecting my ankle's prohibition of steep hills, in any gear. And I love, always, to walk, sometimes around my neighborhood while listening to an Edith Wharton or George Eliot novel on tape; sometimes with my husband, exploring Greenwich Village on one of our sentimental returns to the city where we courted; sometimes on an easy hike up into the Santa Monica Mountains with my sons and their friends. I work with my body now instead of against it, and when the pain advises me to stop, I no longer treat this advice as an obstacle to "work through," but as a vital sign.

*   *   *

The other evening, on our way home from a family dinner out, we passed our blond mystery woman dragging herself up the street. "What do you suppose the rest of her life is like?" my husband asked.

"It hurts to imagine," I replied, reaching for his hand.

Spiraling Down: Overcoming Depression

Regina Anavy

Picture a spiral. You are on top, going along in your usual pattern. A thought intrudes, a moment of doubt, guilt, or self-reproach. Your spirits drop. You descend deeper into the spiral. As your mind turns inward and your thoughts become more constricted, your options seem to narrow. You suddenly flash in vivid detail to every error committed in your past: spiteful words uttered spontaneously that you cannot take back; impulsive acts you cannot erase. You begin to obsess about relationships that have drifted away—all your fault, of course. And you weren't always the perfect child, the perfect sibling, the perfect worker, lover, or friend. Oh, the mistakes you have made. Your life is one big mistake, from the minute you were born. You spiral down and down into the blame and shame of your life.

This negative-feedback loop of depression was a familiar part of my psyche for as long as I can remember. Usually, I would find my way back up and come out on top of the spiral. However, in 1971, my luck ran out and I had a full-blown breakdown.

I was in Cuba, cutting sugarcane with the Fourth Venceremos Brigade. I had volunteer-worked my way up to this point in my radical career by being active in the civil rights movement, the women's movement, and the antiwar movement. I had even become an aboveground member of the Weather Underground through a boyfriend who was involved with the group. It was the perfect time for me to get out of town, since I had inadvertently taken part in an explosion in the U.S. Capitol building. I say "inadvertently" because my friend had surfaced to come visit me and had left a book on my shelf. When he picked it up later, he opened the front cover to show me: The book was hollow inside, and it held blasting caps. No one had been hurt in the explosion, but I still felt guilty about my participation, and I felt guilty about feeling guilty, for that meant I was not a committed revolutionary and still had bourgeois tendencies.

My disillusionment with the Cuban revolution began the moment I arrived in the work camp. The lack of individual rights was apparent. The one newspaper we saw, *Granma*, spelled "America" with a "k." The Cubans did not approve of the gay *brigadistas,* who were considered counterrevolutionary. This was the catchword of the moment, and to be branded as such was the biggest insult imaginable and an invitation to be ostracized. It seemed to me that what was happening in Cuba was unrelated to my cultural values. Such thinking was, of course, counterrevolutionary.

We had a daily routine that provided structure: At sunrise, we had a shot of strong coffee, piled into claustrophobic Soviet trucks, and sang revolutionary songs all the way to the fields. We worked until lunchtime, came back in the trucks (same singing routine, with a few shouted slogans thrown in), had a copious lunch, took a siesta, and went out again in the afternoon. Before each trip to the fields we sharpened our machetes. At night there were cultural activities: movies shown in the "Palm Theater," where we leaned against trunks of felled palm trees. Occasionally, musicians came to perform for us. It was one big revolutionary party.

Social pressure worked subtly in the camp. We were "invited" to show up for work production meetings, where we were lectured on how to increase the amount of cane we cut. Occasionally, some important personage would come through the camp to give us a pep talk. We were expected to drop what we were doing, fall out in military fashion, line the path, and clap enthusiastically. It was like being in a cult.

Unfortunately, before going to Cuba I had become dependent on marijuana to elevate my mood. I had been in psychoanalysis for years, but its tendency to analyze and overanalyze had made me worse. So now here I was, in a physically and emotionally trying situation, sleeping six to a tent, being covered in ash in the cane fields, often cutting myself with the blade of the machete, being harassed by the Cuban overseers who told us to cut faster and aim lower, and without my usual crutch (marijuana was not tolerated in Cuba).

There was also a lot of infighting among the different political factions. Doubt began to creep in, and I started questioning everything. If I had been wrong about the Cuban revolution, was I wrong about other beliefs? I came to the conclusion that I was wrong about everything; my life had been built on a lie. And then I became consumed by all-encompassing guilt for feeling that way. Everyone around me, except for a few of us doubters, seemed to be fully engaged in the revolutionary experience of cutting cane and mouthing the party line. So what was wrong with me? I took it all personally, losing my sense of perspective and, worst of all, my sense of humor.

The Cubans seemed fiercely patriotic and proud of their country, in great contrast with the North Americans' constant criticism of our own government and its policy toward Cuba. I started to feel weird about this, suspecting that the Cubans actually looked down on us for our lack of patriotism. They were also very antihippie and antidrug, and they considered us spoiled and self-indulgent. They were determined to stamp these qualities out of us through hard work and indoctrination. I began to view my critical attitude toward Cuba as a symptom of overwhelming negativity. Was I just a rebel for the sake of rebellion? Was I doomed to see only the bad side of everything?

My self-confidence plummeted and I became more withdrawn, convinced that everyone suspected me of being a CIA agent. For one thing, I was being openly critical; for another, I was taking a lot of photos. The paranoia, both inside the camp and inside my own head, was not helped by the fact that one of the Cubans confided in me that before we had come, the Cuban government had taken them aside to warn them about us North Americans: We would try to seduce them sexually; we would try to poison their minds with our bourgeois, capitalist thinking; we were not really their friends. So it was all a sham—the forced companionship in the camp, the forced solidarity. My identity as a revolutionary was a sham, too, built on a false premise.

My world was falling apart. Going home was not an option, nor was dulling my doubts by smoking grass or going along with the political program. Clearly, I did not belong there, but where *did* I belong? Ironically, I could have bragged about being more revolutionary than anyone because I was involved with the Weather Underground, but the one thing I *could* do was keep a secret, so this was not an option, either.

You realize you are in a prison of your own making. There is a wall separating you from others; how easily those fragile social connections you once took for granted are broken. You have forgotten how to engage in the proper behavior required for making contact. You feel detached from the human race, and this creates more self-blame.

This sense of detachment amid people with whom I could not connect was the worst feeling of all. It was a signal to me that, emotionally, there was no turning back. I was doomed.

Somewhere down the spiral, after Blame, Guilt, and Detachment have arrived in full force, Anxiety suddenly appears. It's a rogue wave, slamming into your body, turning you upside down, and saturating every pore. You are drowning, unable to surface for air. Once Anxiety seeps in, you realize it has been there all along, stalking you, hovering in the background like a rejected lover lurking outside your house, waiting for a moment when your guard is down and you have left a window cracked.

Fear is Anxiety's twin, for you now know there is no escape from your private descent into hell. Sleep, when it comes, is full of nightmares. You awaken in the middle of the night, terrified and filled with disgust at your terror. Morning arrives and you do not feel rested. Time becomes meaningless, for you are wrapped in the time zone of depression, your own private misery. The simplest act becomes a struggle: getting out of bed, brushing your teeth, combing your hair, dressing. Sheer maintenance wears you out. You are alone, falling faster into inner space.

As fear and despair took over, I experienced a loss of self, as if my core identity had been smashed and I had no way of reassembling it. I moved through the days like an automaton. So much of my energy was being taken up in this inner dialogue that little was left for interacting with my *compañeros,* who, sensing my weirdness, began to distance themselves from me. This social isolation caused more anxiety. I was in a repetitive loop of self-criticism, self-loathing, guilt, despair, anxiety, loss of hope, and, finally, thoughts of suicide.

The last two weeks of my Cuba trip were spent touring the island. This included a "forced march" in the Sierra Maestra. It was exhausting. By the time we returned home, in the hold of a ship, I was moving like a zombie, incapable of connecting, except with the other walking wounded. One of them was a drug addict who had spent the whole time in Cuba in a hospital, going through withdrawal. We spoke briefly, standing on deck, leaning against the rail. It was all I could do not to throw myself overboard. I vaguely remember the homecoming and being unable to articulate my experience or connect with my friends. I vaguely remember buying sleeping pills and checking into a hotel. I vaguely remember writing a suicide note, explaining my "logical" reasons for doing this. I do remember the relief of gulping down those pills and lying down on the bed to sleep, forever. But it hurt, and I woke up: I was scared. While unconscious, I had had a vision of going down a tunnel, being led by a rabbit, and the thought had come to me that I was not ready to die. I did not want to follow that rabbit, and I had forced myself to wake up. It was one of the hardest things I had ever done, pushing myself up off the bed and staggering into the hallway, where I incoherently flagged down a hotel guest and then passed out. When I awoke, I was on the locked ward of a hospital, having my stomach pumped. A good-looking young cop was standing over me, smiling, and I knew I was safe.

My first night in the hospital, I was rambling and carrying on, happy to be alive. They put me in solitary until I could calm down. The doctors laughed at me for trying to commit suicide with over-the-counter sleeping pills, and I felt like a failure again. This feeling came and went during the next few weeks. My analyst showed up (he must have felt like a failure himself). The hospital's group-therapy approach was much more directive than his Freudian method. I was surprised by how many of my friends came to visit; some of them sought to "rescue" me, in a guerrilla action, from the evil clutches of conventional medicine, but I knew I needed to be there and refused to go with them.

The one failure in my treatment was that I was not put on antidepressants immediately. The tranquilizers they gave me zonked me out but did nothing to quell my suicidal thought pattern. After three months, I entered a halfway house. This turned out to be a healing experience, and I gradually clawed my way back to mental health.

There were two crucial turning points. First, I learned that I could easily get a gun from one of the other residents, which would make committing suicide a definite possibility. I made a decision to stop thinking about suicide: I had regained my mind. Second, before moving into my own apartment, I had a brief affair with one of the staff, who made me feel like a desirable woman: I had regained my body.

I began to see a different psychiatrist, one with a new approach to the issue of depression. For him, it was simply a matter of proper brain chemistry, and he immediately put me on a tricyclic antidepressant. Amazingly, within two weeks, my energy and zest for life returned, and I became rational and more focused on my future. I was able to make social connections and appropriate decisions without second-guessing everything I did, a state of mind that had immobilized me since my breakdown.

The realization that my lifelong depression had a chemical and even a genetic component (my father had tried to commit suicide twice) relieved me of guilt and despair. I now had hope that I could recover.

And I did. I moved to the West Coast and went to law school for one year. I rented a beautiful apartment and got a job as a legal assistant at a law firm in San Francisco. With the money I saved, I bought property, becoming a real member of the establishment, without any guilt. I became a massage therapist and took classes in painting. I maintained my interest in politics but worked within the framework of the Democratic Party, serving on the State Central Committee for two years. I met a man and fell in love. We traveled the world together, got married, and started what became a successful business.

Since my hospitalization more than three decades ago, I have had other bouts of depression, but I have learned to catch myself at the top of the spiral before I begin that terrifying descent. I heed those first warning signs—self-deprecating thoughts and debilitating anxiety—and, with the help of daily medication, I know I can stop the fall.

In 2003, I became interested in Cuba again and felt brave enough to go back for another look, legally this time. I have returned many times since then to work on environmental and humanitarian projects and to see Cuban friends. I no longer feel guilty about my negative perception of the revolution. If someone called me "counterrevolutionary" today, I would laugh and agree, taking it as a compliment.

Now officially retired, I have many interests that keep me engaged. As I get older, I know the future will hold challenges, and I am confident in my strength to face them.

Kashim Hahayim
Hannah Yakin

In 1956, I developed a rash that spread rapidly over my entire body. Having left my hometown for a secretarial job in Utrecht, I didn't know any doctors. My employer recommended her younger brother, who had recently finished his medical studies and was trying to set up his own practice.

There were no other patients in the waiting room, so I could see the doctor right away. He was young, only a few years older than I.

"I'm not a dermatologist," he said. "But I hope you agree that a good general practitioner should know his way around the literature." With that, he removed a tome from the shelf. As he pored over the pictures and became engrossed in the text, I waited and scratched. After what seemed a long time, he suggested an ointment and asked me to come back in two days.

Impressed by the doctor's candid ways, I returned several times. The rash persisted, so I tried every new ointment and diet he advised. But it only became worse. After a while, he admitted defeat and sent me to a specialist. Thus started my odyssey from one dermatologist to another. When they had tried everything and had consulted every expert in the field—my rash was now nearly unbearable—they sent me to a retired dermatologist who not only took up the challenge, but who was willing to spend as much time on my case as it would take to cure me.

When, in the course of a long interview, I told him I had been in Israel, he suggested that I might have contracted some mysterious Oriental disease in what, for all he knew, was a Levantine, underdeveloped, third-world country. "African parrots are known to carry microbes that cause leishmaniasis or Rose of Jericho," he said.

"But Doctor, Israel is not in Africa," I protested. "And Jericho is not in Israel. And anyway, it's been three years since I was there."

The old man took off his spectacles, smiled, and confessed that he had never looked up the exact location of Israel on the map. He knew it had been created as a homeland for the Jews, but he had always been more interested in skin diseases than in religion. However, since I had been in Israel, he would love to learn everything I could tell him about it. "Some diseases have an incubation period of years," he said. "Maybe something will give me a clue about the possible origins of your problem." He lit a pipe and leaned back in his chair. "Come on," he said. "Start at the beginning and tell me everything you remember."

*   *   *

I had wanted to emigrate to Israel immediately after high school, but my father insisted that I learn a profession first. Although I had an interest in art, I learned typing and shorthand in four languages. After I graduated from secretarial school, I was still determined to go to Israel, but my father worried. He offered me a round-trip ticket if I agreed to see the land with my own eyes, return home, and only then decide if I really wanted to build my future there. It was a very expensive present, and he sacrificed a great deal to buy it. In order to get a reduced fare, a number of young Zionists booked passage on the boat as a group. Once in Israel, we would go our separate ways.

After a sleepless night on the train to Marseille, we sat on our luggage for half a day before boarding the smallest of the three Israeli passenger ships, the *Artsa,* which means "to the land." As soon as we crossed the gangplank, I spotted an enclosed rear deck with two easy chairs. I curled up in one of them and fell asleep so fast that I never noticed leaving Europe. When I opened my eyes, I was looking into the face of a middle-aged man seated in the other chair. "Have you slept well?" he asked in French. I don't remember what I answered, but it must have been funny, because he burst out laughing and declared, "But this is a private deck, young lady. Who do you think you are, falling asleep in the captain's chair?"

"The captain's chair? How was I supposed to know?"

"You climbed over that rope, didn't you?"

"I don't remember. . . ."

"In that case, you must have fallen out of the sky, right into the chair. As it happens, I'm quite pleased you did. May I ask you to keep me company during the voyage out? My name is Yeheskel Sahar. I am the head of Israel's police force and the private guest of our captain, in whose chair you have been sleeping."

I jumped up and exclaimed, "Oh, but the captain may come any moment; I have to hurry. . . . "

Mr. Sahar laughed. "No need to run; he's busy most of the time. Anyway, his deck chair is chiefly a status symbol. I'll ask him to let you use it when he doesn't need it. Does that suit you?"

During those days at sea, Yeheskel Sahar and I were inseparable. Occasionally I even dined with him at the captain's table. I was vaguely aware that the members of my group, among them my foster brother, Josef, regarded me as a snob, but I had no time for them: In the five days that I sat in the captain's deck chair, Yeheskel taught me more about Israel, its history, its problems, and its hopes for the future than I had learned in all my twenty years in Holland. He also taught me my first Hebrew phrase, *kashim hahayim*, "life is difficult." We often said it while staring over the Mediterranean, in the direction of the Promised Land.

Before dawn, on a beautiful morning in June, the *Artsa* arrived in Haifa. All the passengers stood on the deck and watched the sun rise over Mount Carmel. The girls cried with emotion and the boys wrapped themselves in their prayer shawls and recited their morning prayers. Israel's mere existence was a miracle for us, after the Holocaust, which had ended only eight years earlier, and the near annihilation of the Jewish people.

Mr. Sahar was the first to go ashore. An official car was awaiting him at the wharf. Before he disembarked, we shook hands and exchanged a heartfelt *"kashim hahayim."*

Like everybody else in our group, I had a list of addresses of acquaintances and relatives, however distant, compiled by my parents, uncles, aunts, and their friends. Merging my list with Josef's, we mapped a route that covered the entire country, 250 miles from north to south and 12 miles at its narrowest point, 60 at its widest from west to east. Since the telephone book of the three big cities and all the rest comprised no more than a few dozen pages, we didn't make appointments with people we wanted to visit. We simply went there, knocked on their doors, and announced, "I am the daughter or son of such and such, and this is my friend. Can we stay for a few days?" Even if nobody was home when we arrived, we didn't have to wait outside in the burning sun. More often than not, front doors were unlocked. Some people owned an icebox and others placed an earthenware jug filled with water by an open window, so there would always be cool drinks.

Although most of the people we visited shared our background, their opinions and priorities were very different from ours. For example, my mother had always suggested that every policeman was basically a heartless person. She acknowledged that policemen were a necessity but would have been horrified if one of her children had chosen what she considered an unsympathetic profession. By contrast, the Israelis of 1953 were infinitely proud of their Jewish policemen, who dedicated their lives to protecting the Israeli

opped, we went
 the mountains
 their reflection
lor.
ded the *Artsa* for
 seasick most of
 to Amsterdam,
latform.

yself vigorously.
and said he had
king water, sand
 over and would
edication might
ue to use one of

tmare persisted.
l colleagues kept
em.

is quite content
secretary; in the
ade new friends
ies. I never gave
longer in such a

people. The same was true of soldiers and laborers. Of course, my parents had taught me to respect all the professions, but they would not have been happy if one of their children had become a soldier, farmer, or plumber. I myself was keenly aware of being a borderline case, with my certificate from the School for Secretaries. I never doubted that my parents would have preferred a university degree.

The priorities of the people we visited in Israel were at the other end of the spectrum. Either they had fled Europe before the Holocaust, leaving certificates and qualifications behind (along with crystal vases and diamond necklaces), or they had survived concentration camps or spent years hiding in attics, caves, or sewer systems. Some had even arrived in Israel on immigrant ships and had watched the English drown their comrades while in sight of the Promised Land. The survivors no longer cared for worldly possessions, titles, or degrees. All they wanted was a safe place for their children's future. They used to sing, "Happy is the man who builds a road," alluding not to metaphysical roads, but to those of concrete and tar, roads on which their children and grandchildren would walk and drive as free people in their own country.

The Israelis I knew in 1953 loved to receive visitors—not only because we brought firsthand news from friends and family, but also because they, the pioneers, were proud to show us, the newcomers, what they had already accomplished. They were proud of the tomato plant in their back yard and the wild anemones in their front garden; of their two-room flats with concrete floors and whitewashed walls; of their army

beds with threadbare blankets and stra
They were proud to lodge us on the floo
sending us on to their own acquaint
bricklayers elsewhere in the country—so
and understand what it means to build a

In kibbutz Sde Nehemiah, we wer
grade-school teacher who took us on
Lebanese border. His hobby was compilir
dictionary. How we marveled when we he
playing and even quarreling in Hebrew!
I had used my high school years to lear
instead of classical Latin and Greek.

On the boat, Josef had met a member c
who invited him for a visit. We never
invitation included me, which indeed it d
kibbutz had acquired a single radio, which
the communal room for the benefit of al
principle, kibbutz people didn't own priva
some of the families had received prese:
or European relatives. In June 1953, all h
kibbutz Matsuba owned a private radio. I
one of those families received the much-c
Josef and I were visiting. The next day,
assembly where somebody proposed that
radio for the last family who did not have
was accepted unanimously. Josef and I we
this manifestation of pure communism.

Be'er Sheva was surrounded by sand an
itself was nothing but a few houses aroun

Every evening, when the temperature d
out and swam in the Red Sea. I loved to se
glowing red in the last sun rays and castin
in the sea that derives its name from their c

At the end of September, our group boa
the return trip. The sea was rough and I wa:
the time. We took the train from Marseill
where my father was waiting for me on the

* * *

I stopped talking and resumed scratching n
The old doctor thanked me for the story
several clues to work on, such as bad drir
bugs, and scorpions. He had to think thing
call me as soon as he had an idea of what r
cure me. In the meantime, I should contin
my many ointments.

I went home and the dermatological nig
I couldn't work, I couldn't sleep. Friends an
their distance, for fear that I might infect t

* * *

Before I developed that horrible rash, I w
with my life in Utrecht. By day, I worked as
evenings, I studied at the Art Academy. I
and went to the theater and to dance par
up my plans to go to Israel, but I was no

hurry. Whenever I mentioned the subject, there was always somebody to show me how foolish I was. "You will starve intellectually and spiritually," people said. "You want to be an artist. You need the proximity of the big museums, the ancient masterpieces of Rembrandt and Leonardo, places like the Louvre and the Prado. In Israel, they have nothing but a few local daubers. You can't just throw away your education, your culture. Your dreams are romantic but unrealistic."

And later, when my rash was at its worst, they added, "Now you see! What would you have done with your pimples, all alone at the other end of the world?"

One day, I happened to walk past the office of the young doctor I had first consulted. I went in and had to wait only a few minutes before being admitted. Sitting in front of his desk, I broke down completely. Crying, I told him what all the specialists had said, and how even the old dermatologist, who had been so dedicated to my cause, had not been able to help me.

The doctor looked at the ceiling for a long time, uttered a deep sigh, and said, "I will ask you one question and you must answer quickly, without taking the time to think about your answer. Are you ready?"

By this time, so many physicians had interrogated me on so many occasions that I could answer their questions automatically. Resigned, I waited. The doctor leaned forward and asked, "What do you want most in your life?"

Without hesitating, I responded, "To go to Israel."

"Then go," he said.

I went.

I arrived at my destination with tons of advice and a suitcase full of ointments I never used. I can't remember how or when I was cured, but I have been in Israel for the last fifty years and my rash has never returned.

I am sadly aware that many things have changed. What in 1953 was Israel's future has by now become her past. Israel's childhood was like my passage on the *Artsa* with Yeheskel Sahar: too good to be true, impossible to follow up. Nevertheless, as long as it lasted, it was great. Unforgettable, even.

We Israelis have not been able to keep our hands off the apple of good and evil. Paradise has been lost and lost again, but I am still here, for better or worse. For whatever people may think of us Jews, one thing is sure: We need a land of our own.

Although I have lived a good life, the winged words *kashim hahayim,* "life is difficult," have been on my lips almost daily, and I have never forgotten my friend Yeheskel Sahar, who taught them to me.

How happily surprised we both were when we met by complete coincidence in 1989. By that time, the former chief of the Israeli police force was an old widower with eye problems, and I was the mother and grandmother of a large clan. We reminisced for a while about our voyage on the *Artsa.* When it was time to say goodbye, we shook hands and he said, "If I had been smart back in 1953, I would have married you."

But that, I guess, is neither here nor there.

Some Other Day

Kate Maloy

The phone rings and I reach for it, annoyed. I've been working on my essay for this book, and I'm still writing as I pick up. I don't recognize the caller's voice, but I hear a strangled quality and realize she's no telemarketer. She introduces herself as the daughter of D, who is married to my ex-husband. Why isn't D calling? Her daughter explains—and blows to pieces my sweetly serious essay. My heart, too.

Such news should come only from a loved one, but in this case the loved one is dead, and I must be told so that I can continue the telling.

So that I can tell my son, just days before his twenty-first birthday, that his father, P, has died. That he has shot himself.

*   *   *

First, I have to regain my equilibrium, for the news provokes big, gasping sobs and dreadful anger. How could he? With his son finally emerging from a long struggle? With D in the next room? How *could* he! I am staggered by my reaction, for I've been expecting this news for at least twenty-five years.

It takes hours for the overpowering emotions to subside, and when they do I'm dashed by images as thick as a blizzard on a windshield. No sooner does one gust of memories blow away than another clouds my vision. These are vivid, colorful, and contradictory, like P himself.

*   *   *

He rode at the edge of the precipice his whole life, starting at ten, when he nearly died of polio. He recovered intact, except for the use of his right arm. With determined grace, he mastered his left side, learning through the years to make one hand serve as two for drying his back, filling his pipe, knotting a necktie, chopping vegetables. To clean crumbs from a table, he'd use the side of his hand to push them to the edge, then cup his palm under and sweep the crumbs into it with his thumb. To applaud, he would put his good hand beneath his paralyzed hand and slap it up and down.

P lived large, both physically and emotionally. He was excessive in his pursuit of pleasure, whether food, drink, cars, sex, or spending beyond his means. His speech was voluble, undisciplined, profane, and filled with brilliant metaphors he plucked from nowhere. Grand gestures and sweeping emotion fulfilled something in him, releasing explosive laughter or sentimental tears. He wept at Irish music, especially if he had drunk a good bit of Irish whiskey, or beer, or both. He bought the beer by the keg and kept it on tap in a cooler; he kept the whiskey in a crystal decanter. He smoked his pipe nonstop, and the smell of Balkan Sobranie permeated the house even when he wasn't home, for he would leave the tin open to dry the tobacco to his taste.

This was the side of P that the world saw most, the open-hearted hedonist, entertainer, and companion. He gave himself tirelessly to his colleagues, friends, and university students, who adored him. I saw less of him than they did— and more, too. I saw less of his generosity and humor and more of his melancholy, self-doubt, and anger. I was the one who heard him bellow and storm. From anyone else I'd have feared abuse, but P abused only himself. He was his own harshest judge, always on the verge of imposing the death penalty. He talked of suicide for nearly all of our eighteen years together.

The only excess P ever gave up was alcohol, but work quickly ballooned into the void. He was driven; he could not set boundaries. His university benefited greatly, for he established a new department, brought in sterling faculty, and won grant after grant—but then could not stay on top of any of it. He was eternally frantic about unmet deadlines and contracts. At home, beset by the world that he unwittingly *invited* to beset him, he would shout out his rage at its demands, threatening either to check himself into a hospital, so people would leave him alone, or to check himself out, permanently.

*   *   *

When P hit his forties, his high-test life began taking a noticeable toll. Everything he had taken for granted, including the strength of his good limbs and the bottomless energy of his mind, began to wane. He was sure he had some degenerative nerve disease, and he declaimed loudly about this, panicked by his symptoms. I was skeptical, given his tendency to exaggerate, but I was wrong and he was right. Not long after the same symptoms were first seen among other polio survivors, P was diagnosed with post-polio syndrome. The cause remains unknown, but the condition is marked by a slow wasting of neurons and muscles that have stayed healthy for decades after the initial disease. P's tree-trunk legs had lost 40 percent of their muscle mass by the time he was diagnosed. His racquetball and running days were soon over.

It took much longer for our marriage to end. I stayed for our son, our history, and all we had been through. I stayed out of love, exasperation, and stubbornness. I stayed until it was clear that P was not going to slow down, even to save his life. I couldn't watch the self-destructive spiral anymore. It was destroying me, too, and I was determined that it would not destroy our son.

My last stab at saving the marriage was to talk P into counseling. The suicide threats came out right away, and the first thing the therapist did was ask him to promise never to kill himself without telling me first. P promised, and I fell apart. I had thought I was steeled against whatever might happen, but I sobbed with relief.

*   *   *

P kept a loaded gun as a talisman. He used to say that every time he looked at it, he deliberately chose not to use it. Until, of course, he did use it.

And that's another thing I see, with the smoke of decades clearing—that P was *always* choosing to use that gun. It was a foregone conclusion, a thing that had its own ponderous pace and timing, but a thing that was inevitable. A man does not say, every day of his life, *I choose not to kill myself this day,* unless he means, consciously or not, to kill himself some other day.

*   *   *

When P married D, I was glad. The new marriage didn't slow his physical decline, but it brought him the compassion and love that sustained him, especially when he had to give in and buy a motorized wheelchair for daily mobility. His legs remained just strong enough to get him in and out of the chair, the shower, his bed and clothing, but it was time to save them from unnecessary wear. He lived in terror of the day when he would be forced to surrender to others his most intimate care.

That day approached slowly, through a long series of falls, near falls, bruises, and stitches. It finally arrived in August 2006, when P fell again and broke a vertebra. The damage wasn't severe enough to warrant surgery, but he faced a long recovery, during which he would indeed have to rely on the care of others.

My first thought was that he would make his exit right away. He couldn't sit upright without a brace, and he couldn't put the brace on by himself. Pain pills were messing with his insides, and the loss of his salary—he wouldn't be able to teach for at least a semester—was messing with his head. Soon, however, he was bragging about the speed of his recovery. He quickly took back most of his own care, and he sounded upbeat in email messages and phone calls, full of plans for a blog and for a family reunion, a chance for our son to reunite with aunts, uncles, and cousins. He asked me whether my novel would be out in time for Christmas.

A pair of clerical errors abruptly changed all that. The first denied disability benefits that P was indeed entitled to. The second, a hospital claim submitted to the wrong insurer, held up payment of his medical bills. Neither was an insurmountable problem, but P couldn't make the climb to surmount them. He killed himself only hours after he got the news.

*   *   *

This is why the promise he made to me was impossible. A friend—also a clinical psychologist—calmed my anger by explaining that suicide is the result of a total loss of control, not to mention profound underlying depression. The pain that pushes a person completely over the edge is so powerful that it obscures everything else, including love, including the desire to protect a son, including the horror that would normally keep him from inflicting unspeakable trauma upon his wife and dreadful loss upon his friends and family.

My son somehow knew this. He told me he believed his father's suicide was a "spontaneous act that was a long time coming." His insight—evidence that he was finding ways to understand and integrate what had happened—further diminished my anger but didn't entirely dispel it. It still washed over me at unpredictable moments. It drew upon the anger in which my marriage to P had dissolved, and it drowned for a while the effort we had made to remain friends so that our son would never feel guilty toward either of us for loving the other.

*   *   *

I struggled with anger until coincidence, or the cosmos, intervened. A week after P's death, at the first moment I could "afford" to be laid low, I dropped. This was after I had talked often with my son, who was in California. He assured me that he was coping and had good friends close by. For the first time in five painful years—from midadolescence to the beginnings of adulthood—he was working, well paid, and living where he wanted to. Before P's death, he had been briefly, truly happy. Now he was trying to absorb his loss in manageable increments. We both knew it would take years.

My illness came on with belly pains like swords. I waited three days, thinking I had some virulent flu that would resolve itself. When it didn't, my husband took me to the local clinic, a service run by two nurse-practitioners in our small coastal town. They ordered tests and told me I had pancreatitis. That was on a Thursday. When I went back on

Monday, the pain was worse. I'd eaten almost nothing in a week, and what I did eat came right back up.

The NPs consulted a gastroenterologist, who told them to send me to the ER twenty-five miles north. Once there, I couldn't sit or stand, so I lay on the floor of the waiting room, vomiting into what looked like a blue plastic tube sock, while my husband kept checking at the desk.

Finally, abdominal x-rays and a CT scan showed not pancreatitis but a bowel obstruction. Attendants bundled me into an ambulance, which took me over back roads to a larger, better equipped hospital about fifty miles inland. Two days later I underwent surgery, followed by six more days in the hospital.

*   *   *

Illness took me across territory less desolate than P's but bordering on the same country. Along the way, I thought about him and tried to glimpse some shadow of his earthly self as he had faced that last injury and those last treatments. I saw him buckle under the final straws piled on so casually by the medical bureaucracy. Against my will, I saw his violent final gesture, repeatedly. I heard him bellow at the universe: *No more!*

Was he afraid? Had death ever frightened him, or had he always, like John Keats, been half in love with it for its promise of ease? I'll never know, but that doesn't keep the questions from haunting me—and sending me back to what I do know.

I know that P saw other children die of polio and felt lucky to lose only one arm. I know, too, that his father, P Senior, was determined to squelch any self-pity in his son or any notion that he was crippled. Even after his father left his mother a year later, P continued to idealize him.

Before polio, P had been a healthy, sturdy boy with every reason to believe in a benign universe. Afterward, he was much more vulnerable. He had seen too much, had almost died, and had been separated from his family for six months while in the hospital. From the moment he got home, he was expected to soldier on and stanch his fears and grief. He did the best he could, and he tried from then on to emulate his father's easy charm and underlying, almost military steel.

He succeeded too well. I believe that's how he developed his two faces—the public, smiling, funny, and generous face, and the private one that agonized and doubted and couldn't turn its gaze from death for long.

How morbidly fortuitous, then, that his father killed himself, in his sixties, ostensibly for financial reasons. He might as well have issued an invitation for his son to follow him one day, and perhaps this was why P so steadfastly defended his father's suicide. He insisted that he understood it, just as he had understood his father's long-ago defection to that other woman. P was never angry with his father. He saw the man's suicide as a rational response to an intolerable problem.

I would give anything to ask P now—or to *have* asked him, years ago—if he thought he had been spared unjustly when he survived polio. Did his father unintentionally reinforce this damning idea, first when he was so strict with P, and again when he left his family for someone with healthy children? Was P a victim of survivor guilt? I know his thoughts of suicide began early. He once told me he'd come very close in his twenties.

These reflections came during a period of weeks and finally took away my anger, all of it, from the past and from P's refusal of a future. What emerged then was—is—profound sadness and all the compassion I couldn't muster when it might have helped. Yes, I had reason to be angry all those years. I couldn't make myself heard above P's depression and anxiety. I was powerless and understandably resentful, but I wish I could have seen beyond my anger then.

Anger, like any form of pain, is a signal that something is wrong. The challenge is to diagnose the cause, which I couldn't do until illness, aging, and time cracked open first P's denial and then my own. Under his father's misguided instruction, P learned to deny and suppress his childhood losses and pain. He took the lesson so deeply to heart that it shaped his life, leading to serious depression, which he also denied until it was too late. P's denial cost him his life.

I, too, denied pain, burying it not in depression but in anger, which was easy to justify but was a blindfold. My underlying problem was fear—not only that P would self-destruct, but that I would be shattered. Anger was my defense. I never let myself feel the pain of our lost connection or his desperation until D's daughter called. She barely got her words out before that old pain woke up screaming. So did new anger, but this time its source was clear—I was outraged, and terrified, that P and his father had left a seeming legacy of suicide for the next in line. For my son.

My son, however, had recently been the one to teach me an important lesson about fear. We'd been talking about our changing relationship, about how we were gradually becoming more like friends and equals than parent and child, even though my maternal feelings and protectiveness persisted. I had already acknowledged, a few years back, that he would, and must, make his own decisions and take the consequences if he chose wrong. In our recent conversation, though, I also confessed that I still worried desperately about his well-being.

He looked at me and said quietly, using a Quaker expression he'd grown up with, "I wish you wouldn't do that. It's the opposite of holding someone in the light." He was right. I had been holding him in the dark of my worst fears, and I promised instead to envision him bathed in light, thriving, happy, loving, and loved.

I've kept that promise through the ordeals that have followed it. The family pattern of suicide is by far the hardest to face down, but I do so by reminding myself that my son is his own person, not his father or grandfather, and that he also has a different legacy from me than from his father. Other fears—that my illness might orphan my son in a terrible one-two punch, that my husband would exhaust himself with worry, that the belly pains would never stop—came and went until the ambulance ride.

Every bump was another sword. I had a tube in my nose that went down my throat to my stomach and made me gag. My husband hadn't been permitted to ride with me. I was scared and miserable. Then I saw in a flash that *everything* was out of my hands—the skill of the ambulance driver, the outcome of my illness, all of it, even my son's fate. I surrendered, just like that, just like grace, and in the blissful relief that followed, nothing would have been easier than to slip into the warm dark. I wasn't ready to go, but I believed for the first time that I will be, one day.

* * *

Strangely, that sudden, revelatory letting go brought to mind Dylan Thomas's contrary refrain: "Do not go gentle into that good night / Old age should burn and rage at close of day." I was amused to think how young Thomas was when he wrote that. He died young, too, of alcoholism and other excesses, raging and reveling all the way. No doubt he'd have saluted P's dramatic departure.

I think it is the young who are most fond of Thomas's defiant notions, though there are exceptions. Keats, for example, knew the tug of a peaceful death, having suffered a long time from the tuberculosis that finally killed him in his twenties. Perhaps it was illness, as opposed to addiction and wild living, that made death his friend. Who knows? Perhaps Keats had read William Blake's poem "Eternity": "He who binds himself to a joy / Doth the winged life destroy. / He who kisses the joy as it flies / Lives in eternity's sunrise." Both Thomas and P bound themselves to "joys" that later killed them. Keats apparently preferred the sunrise.

In any case, the old can learn from Keats, as I have learned from my son, that the light shines brightest in the absence of clutching, fearing, and resisting. At sixty-two, my goal is to embrace old age as a hard-earned blessing and a ripe time of life—one that is meant to be lived for itself, in the moment, and not in fear of the end that draws closer.

If I manage this—if I use my remaining days well and do not go mad in the welter of youth-obsessed media, cosmetics, surgeries, and pharmaceuticals—it will be a consequence of good fortune more than virtue. I believe we play the hand we are dealt. We have some choice in how we do this, but less than we like to suppose. The hand is what it is. This, too, I saw when I journeyed through illness and watched P on his different path. I recovered; he did not. That in no way impugns him or ennobles me.

*　*　*

I picture him reading over my shoulder and wonder if he objects that I've made public so many aspects of his life and death. I don't think so, for his suicide leaves a difficult burden on all who survive him. He has made his exit and found his peace. Now the rest of us must confront both his pain and our own. The struggle is our bequest from him, and how we manage it is our story. It belongs to each of us to tell as we see fit. It is how we heal—something P could never do.

My story of P and his untimely death ends with this: I am forever grateful that I knew him, and I will always love him in my odd and shifting fashion. I am equally grateful that I left him when I did, for, as my son has said, P and I both found true love soon after. P found D, and I found my husband, who is steadily loving and has only one face, dear and familiar.

Truth, In the Middle

Deborah Grabien

It's not quite seven in the morning and I'm sitting at the computer. There's a cup of very dark coffee off to one side, just out of reach of two enormous cats who both want to be in my lap at once. It's clear outside the window, not all that common in San Francisco this early in the day. Usually I'd expect the marine layer to have left ground fog, covering my car and my roses.

I'm up so early because, like the man in whose voice I'm writing, I've had a bad night. Last night was the weekly shot of interferon I take to keep my multiple sclerosis under some sort of control. Without it, I'd probably spend a lot of time using a cane or possibly be mostly forced to use a wheelchair. So yes, the interferon is necessary and useful, but that doesn't make the occasional inexplicably adverse reaction any easier to deal with. Chronic illness came late in my life, and, lacking belief in a theology to tell me otherwise, I'm disinclined to be thankful for any level of pain at all. As far as I'm concerned, all pain is miserable.

At the moment, I'm working. Between sips of coffee, I'm letting John Peter "JP" Kinkaid, the protagonist and narrator of my new series, the *Kinkaid Chronicles*, react to the discovery that his longtime, much younger lover, Bree Godwin, has been diagnosed with cervical cancer.

> *Somewhere inside the middle-aged lioness was a frightened teenager. And there was nothing—not one damned thing—I could do to help, not this time. The feeling was about as bad as it gets in this life, and I suddenly found myself thinking, This is what she lives with, this feeling, dealing with my MS, with my heart murmur, with all my health issues. This is what she lives with, every day, waking and sleeping. How does she do it? How can she deal. . . ?*

I end up pushing both cats off my lap. Right now the soles of my feet are tingling and roaring, and any weight on my thighs is agony. I find myself rereading a scene in the third book of the *Chronicles*, titled *London Calling*. JP, aging rocker, English expat, and multiple sclerosis patient, is talking about the day he was diagnosed with MS.

> *I remember that I'd been calm, or at least I thought I was calm. That was probably because Bree wasn't. She was completely freaked, on the edge of disintegrating. I'd never seen her this way, and I couldn't deal at all. I'd had an instinct, even back then, that on those rare occasions when she was going to need the space to fall apart, I had to pick up the slack, you know? Only way to do it was staying calm.*

Bree is a dozen years JP's junior, and they've been a couple since she was seventeen. She's not only his lover, she's his caregiver and his personal cook and his bodyguard and his amanuensis. The hallmark of their relationship, its foundation, is that, from the moment they came together, she's been the tough one. JP has spent a quarter century in a state of passive aggression, enabled by Bree's fierce protectiveness, her desire to keep the world at bay and make his life easy.

And now here they are in a situation where he's the one affected by the reality behind the bad news—and finally, the weight becomes too much, and she cracks.

They don't let Bree come back with me for the MRI procedure itself, which I suppose is just as well. She's as tough as they're made, but she doesn't like needles and she's mildly claustrophobic. She also doesn't deal well with the idea of anything being less than perfect for me, so between the dye injections and watching me disappear head first into the bowels of the MRI machine, she'd have completely flipped her shit.

JP Kinkaid exists because thirty-plus years ago, when I was a fierce teenager, I knew and loved an extraordinary man. The man who gives me JP's voice didn't have multiple sclerosis; he had other chronic health issues, an illness that would end up killing him at fifty.

He's been dust for many years now. The time we had, the memory of that love, were lost to me for too many years. Now, four years into my own official diagnosis of a midlife built around the day-to-day realities imposed by suffering from a chronic illness, and around trusting the man who loves me to be willing to do for me what I once did for his predecessor, something radical is happening: I'm getting those memories back.

There's a side effect. With the memories come a certain hindsight, things that are always going to be clearer in middle age than they were at the time. The problem, the real killer of this midlife illumination, is that it's too late to do anything about it.

One of the main things I've come to understand about the reality of how I dealt with his illness is that I was too young to understand any of it. Looking back, with these sharp and perhaps overly self-critical eyes, I'd add that he made it more difficult for me. He masked a lot of it, not least because of an alcohol addiction that added an unspeakable complication to the situation. Knowing I'd disapprove, he hid it from me.

I coped, I dealt, I burned, I tried to protect, but for the entire five years, I honestly didn't have the first clue about what he lived with: heart, digestive, lung, and kidney problems, alcoholism. I loved him; that was genuine. But I was working blind to protect him, and I was too—what? Young, prickly, angry?—to understand something very basic: There are times when protection is not what's needed, when building walls can mean shutting yourselves away from each other. There are times when all the walls do is isolate.

That realization, for me, has been the emotional equivalent of a hammer blow to the skull. It's left me with a constant, nagging, bitchy voice that echoes in my head, repeating over and over things like: *Nothing you did for him was any use, you didn't understand what it was like for him, nothing you did for him was any use.*

Oh, that voice, so sly, so relentless, so damned accusing. *Nothing you did for him was any use.*

One thing I haven't sorted out yet is whether the voice is right or wrong. After all, it's not as if I were passive: I held his head in my lap while he shivered, going cold turkey on a nasty mix of codeine, heroin, and cocaine. I emptied nine bottles of hard liquor I'd found secreted around the house, smashed eight of them, kept the ninth, and threatened to christen his skull with it if I ever found a fresh bottle in the house. I bullied him into hospital visits, visits he hated but needed to stay alive. During most of this, I was barely eighteen.

Did any of it help? I don't know, not yet. Maybe the voice is right; maybe it's not. These days, I'm staying sane by taking the position that the truth—as truth so often is—is probably somewhere in the middle.

I'm no stranger to illness or physical pain, either. Beginning with diphtheria when I was too young to remember, I've had half a century of my own health issues. When he and I first came together, I was recovering from a horrifying car accident that left me with more than thirty fractures. Both ankles, one elbow, one knee, and seven fingers subsequently needed to be rebuilt. Like my avatar, Bree, I'm a cervical cancer survivor. I've nearly died on more than one occasion from anaphylactic shock, reacting to life-threatening allergens.

The MS, in fact, is simply the most recent in a string of illnesses and conditions, many part of an autoimmune system that's been compromised since birth. There are days when I picture an invisible queue outside my door, diseases and conditions that have taken a number from a machine and are just waiting in a line to get in and nail me.

So here comes that voice again, whispering away gleefully: *Damn, honey, you were a screwup, how could you not have gotten what it was like for him, stop using being barely nineteen as an excuse, you've been sick your whole life, damn, honey you were a screwup. . . .*

I don't tell the voice to shut the hell up and go away, because, again, that's part of retrieving what was lost: You have to take the shadow along with the light. The fact is, there's solid worth, things I need and want to know, buried in those ugly dark patches. But again, I think the truth is somewhere in the middle. When did the protectiveness help? When did it handicap? What, of anything I ever did or tried to do for him during those periods when he was abusing his already decimated health, had any effect at all?

I cooked for him. Of everything in the long, debilitating march that began with his contracting rheumatic fever as an adolescent, his damaged digestion was his most constant source of pain. He ate little and stayed painfully thin.

And I know how to cook; I've always known how to cook. I'd cooked for my father, the Type 1 diabetic, since I was ten years old. My father loved what I cooked and baked. When even the best store-bought food couldn't tempt him—my mother overcooked everything and disapproved of herbs and spices—he'd come to me for soup, for a decently medium-rare chop, for something with taste that he could digest. A few years later, that math seemed simple: If I could do it for my father, surely I could do it for my lover. I told myself, back then, that I alone could get him to eat.

Now, more than thirty years later and with digestive problems of my own, I look back and cringe. The little voice is sardonic and amused: *Arrogant much? Finally figured it out, did we? You overbearing fool, he had no appetite because it hurt to eat, you probably drove him nuts, he ate tiny bites of what you cooked, even when digesting anything felt like he'd eaten razor blades, and he did it to please you or maybe just to get you to shut up and leave him alone. . . .*

Truth, somewhere in the middle. It's become a mantra.

I've made Bree Godwin a chef and a caterer. This is the first time I've ever put myself into my own fiction. As I write the *Chronicles*, my Land of What If, my journey back to a turning point in my history and his, I'm trying to accomplish a lot more than just writing some damned good fiction. I'm questing, in fact, to see him properly, to get him back, by using his voice. I'm using his eyes to see myself as I was. I'm using his voice to tell me what he saw.

And the little voice, damn it, keeps muttering: *Jesus wept, you were a pain in the ass, you're lucky he didn't strangle you, if someone were as smothering toward Present Day You as you were with 1970s Him, you'd either run off screaming or beat them like a gong.*

Truth in the middle. Lather, rinse, repeat.

* * *

One thing has become clear to me recently: As in many things, I'm out of step with other women of my age in this society. I don't have any body-image demons, and I've never not loved my body. I don't need to be convinced to "accept" my body. To use my favorite vernacular, my body rocks.

The way I've always seen it is, my body carries my heart and mind and spirit around. The visible bits look quite nice, at least to me. In its day, my body's been capable of everything from typing 140 words a minute on a familiar keyboard to making a tourniquet to baking bread to kicking a would-be aggressor in the chin to achieving effortless multiple orgasms. What's not to love?

The message aimed at women my age seems predicated on a different assumption: Its starting point is that women hate their bodies, and that, as they age, they must learn to accept and love those bodies. This leaves me bewildered, because I'm apparently doing things backward once again: After half a century of fiercely loving my body, the old machine is letting me down, becoming angry and unfamiliar and uncooperative.

That's the MS. The fact that the illness—for which there is no cure, and none on the horizon in my lifetime—showed up just as perimenopause kicked in is a nasty trick to have played on me. The disease is unrelenting, reminding me on a daily basis that I can't ever take it lightly.

For one thing, I'm a lifelong endorphin junkie, used to working out on a daily basis. These days, between the MS and the charming development of something called "frozen shoulder," my six hundred daily crunches are down to a hundred that hurt in all the wrong ways; my leg exercises are usually done with the shakes; and my upper-body regimen is completely forbidden for the next two years or until the shoulder condition rights itself, whichever happens first. Am I having fun yet?

Like the younger me she reflects, Bree likes her body. I gave her a nice moment, a reality check that actually felt good to write. The scene is their wedding night, and Bree's wearing the blue velvet dress she wore the first time she slept with JP. Or at least he thinks that's what she's wearing. He finds out otherwise when he realizes the dress has one crucial difference: The original had a zipper as well as buttons down the back.

> *"Oh, honey, I'm a few pounds heavier than I was the first time I let you ravish me." She turned her head, looking at me over her shoulder; her face was bright with laughter, but her eyes were clear shining green, her sexual 'on' signal. "The original is in my closet, at home—it didn't fit nearly as nicely as it did when I was sixteen. So I had an exact copy of the dress made—well, not quite exact."*

I love that scene. Obviously, I gave them a happy ending that the man and I never had a chance at. It was well after I'd written it that I realized something: JP doesn't give a single damn that Bree is ten pounds heavier than she was at seventeen. It never even occurs to him to care. What he cares about is getting her out of that damned dress, even though it means undoing every button. In that scene, he's fifty-five years old and she's forty-three.

The bitchy little voice was silent on that one. As a matter of fact, it's been getting progressively quieter. The steadier I hold the light on who I was and who I am, the more silent and less frequent the voice seems to get.

So I wonder if I'm on the verge of forgiving my younger self for a few things. In the Land of What If, I know I am; heaven knows, that light I've been shining on Bree has made me understand that, then and now, I've been too hard on my younger self. The world of Right Here, Right Now is a different place, though. Forgiving myself in real time may not be quite as easy or cathartic as forgiving my avatars, either his or mine.

A good friend told me that the fact that Younger Me couldn't save him was my tragedy, not my crime. Maybe she's right. That particular light is the brightest one I've got, and it's tricky to aim properly. It keeps wanting to shy away from the road ahead, away from living with chronic illness, away from the fact that I have to do now what the man may or may not have done then: trusting the person who loves me to stick it out.

But the road behind is similar to the one I'm on. The difference is in the players and in the people coping. I'll never know if he forgave me for not understanding how it was for him, for being too young to see it. I'll never know if he even held that against me in the first place. I suspect not: There wasn't a mean bone anywhere in that frail, damaged body of his.

And, of course, it's quite possible—although I haven't reached the point of believing it—that the love wasn't one-directional. For a long time, maybe too long, I've believed the love I felt was never returned. It would be splendid to believe I was wrong about that.

I want to forgive myself for those long-ago mistakes, to forgive my present-day self for getting sick in the first place. I want to find that one spot in the road, the rest stop, the place where I'm neither blinded by the light nor afraid to peer into the shadows.

My money's on its being somewhere in the middle.

Afghanistan

Masha Hamilton

We were rattling across central Afghanistan, following some meager intimation of a road as the CD player blared a Pakistani love song, when three women appeared from nowhere. They rose out of the deserted valley in a loose group, their bodies and faces hidden within floating burqas. They looked like ethereal, sky-blue apparitions. Until, that is, they began waving frantically and running toward us, suddenly and desperately human.

My companion, Massoud Mayar, steered toward them, slowed, and stopped. As they reached us, to my surprise, it was I in the passenger seat toward whom they dove, reaching through the open window, their voices rich like rain falling in the desert. They implored, barely pausing to breathe as they bent and swayed and pointed to their bellies, backs, and chests with hands that moved like tiny wounded birds. I didn't know Pashto beyond a few cursory phrases. But even without the benefit of shared language, I knew what they were saying. Their hidden bodies were still bodies—female bodies that carted and carried and bled, that contained new life and then nurtured it or, too often, buried it. And now those bodies were failing them in some way—an odd bulge on a shoulder, an ache in a hip, an unceasing pain in a belly.

"They think you're the doctor," Massoud said, smiling. "They want you to fix it."

For a second I felt overwhelmed and tried to somehow explain: I'm a writer, with little in the way of tools to understand the medical origins of bodily swellings or pain. But then I reminded myself that I'm also a neophyte shiatsu practitioner, training to be intuitive through my hands, so I pushed open the door of the Russian-made jeep and reached to touch them through their tentlike burqas near the places that troubled them, murmuring something vaguely soothing. In response to my touches, they moved closer, almost climbing into the jeep with me.

Massoud shooed them away, and I waved a bit helplessly as we drove on.

*   *   *

I went to Afghanistan in 2004 to do some reporting on the situation for women. I wanted to see how improved, or not, conditions were. While there, I interviewed women in prison in Kabul and Kandahar, child brides, war widows, and others. This was a "day off," and Massoud had offered to show me his village of Sheik Yassin.

The real doctor the women in burqas were looking for was Roshanak Wardak, Massoud's cousin. When we arrived at his family home, she wasn't yet there, but already more women were waiting, a huddle of perhaps two dozen squatting in the courtyard, some with babies or toddlers in tow. Dr. Roshanak, as she is known, comes every Friday to her cousin's home. And so each Friday, sixty or seventy women who are pregnant, elderly, or ill walk for many miles, down mountains and across valleys, some starting before dawn, to bring their ailments to her door. It sounds like a lot of effort to see a doctor, but they feel lucky to have her and, comparatively, they are.

Here are two examples that might demonstrate just how lucky. At the edge of Kabul, I visited a family in their two-room house cobbled together from war rubble. The father, a former lemon seller, lay on the floor, sick for two months, unseen by any doctor and steadily getting worse, treated only by Tylenol and Tums, the medicines his wife and two daughters managed to gather from aid agencies. And outside Kandahar, I met a matriarch who lived with her four opium-farming sons, their wives, and her twenty-three grandchildren. She had a growth on her lower back the size of a baseball and an intuition that the lump would kill her. But doctors? There were none, she said, who knew how to treat what ailed her. As she spoke, she fingered a cloth from Mecca that she said was to be her death shroud.

So, no matter that these women had walked for hours, and waited for more hours, to have fifteen minutes with Dr. Roshanak; she was still a piece of a luxury in this isolated, impoverished province southwest of Kabul.

Massoud was showing me around his family home when Dr. Roshanak arrived. With an immediate smile, she greeted her cousin, shook my hand, and swept into a small "company" room that doubled as her examining area. I followed to ask a few questions while she drank a quick cup of sweet tea.

She told me her story hurriedly and in shorthand, as though it bored her, as though she didn't notice me trying to soak up every word. Unlike Massoud, who fled to Pakistan during the Taliban period, Dr. Roshanak stayed in Afghanistan and proved to be stronger than one of the world's most repressive regimes of the 1990s.

Imagine that time: Women were permitted in public only fully concealed in burqas and only in the company of a male relative. To expose a wrist or an ankle or varnish one's nails was to risk being beaten for violating the Taliban's strict interpretation of Islam. To be found alone with a man not in one's family would likely result in being stoned or shot to death in Kabul's football stadium during weekly public executions, at which spectators often ate popcorn. One morning, just to demonstrate that they meant business, the Taliban hung human limbs from lampposts and street signs in Kabul, where they remained, rotting in the sun, for several days.

Dr. Roshanak met this intransigence with some of her own. She refused the burqa, wearing instead loose clothing and a headscarf that left her face and dark green eyes fully visible. And she often traveled without male accompaniment to treat women patients. She flaunted the rules—and got away with it.

"They needed me," she explained. "The Taliban needed *some* women doctors to treat their wives and daughters—they weren't going to let a male physician do it. I knew I was the only female doctor in the province. So I told them, 'I don't touch your politics and you don't touch my work. And if you make me wear a burqa, I will stop working.'"

With reluctant Taliban consent, Dr. Roshanak opened a clinic in her home and continued traveling to see patients. Thus began the Friday visits to her cousin's home and the weekly parade of covered women needing to be seen.

* * *

Being *seen*—intimately and superficially, physically and spiritually—is perhaps as basic a human need as food and love. It is a need the burqa denies. The big blue tent, as I came to think of it, makes it impossible to discern a woman's expression—let alone her features—and difficult to hear her voice. Because it is so restraining, its wearer feels less free in both a physical and a psychological sense. My own experiences wearing the burqa in Afghanistan were disorienting: I felt not only like an impostor, but clumsy and off balance and neutered. More restrictive than the hijab, a long scarf that covers the head and shoulders, or the chador, which covers all but the eyes, the burqa conceals a woman's entire face, permitting her to see only through a small rectangular mesh panel that reminded me of the blinders trainers put on horses to keep them under control.

These days, the educated women of Kabul who wear headscarves refuse to pull on the burqa because they often consider it an emblem of the repressive Taliban regime. Many also believe it symbolically weakens the still-eroded position of Afghan women, who, Taliban or no, often must continue to struggle within their homes and communities for the right to be educated, hold jobs, or vote.

But the burqa may be one of the most politicized and misunderstood articles of female apparel ever. Westerners who viewed it as an evil destined to vanish once the Taliban were routed clearly failed to understand its complexity. As proof: Outside of Kabul, the majority of women still wear the burqa. Many, along with their men, believe it is a sign not only of a woman's morality, but also of her innate and dizzying beauty. The female body, according to this way of thinking, is too precious and alluring to be revealed to the world at large. Less romantically, some also believe it keeps women safer in a country sometimes said to resemble the Wild West. The burqa continues to hold powerful sway over Afghan society, affecting both how a woman views her physical self and how she is viewed by others.

*   *   *

When I mentioned to Dr. Roshanak the women Massoud and I had met on the way, and then my own shiatsu training, she brightened visibly. I had received two years of instruction in the traditional Oriental therapy, sometimes also called acupressure. Proponents believe shiatsu can heal physical and psychological ailments, but even naysayers say it feels good and relieves stress. Dr. Roshanak needed no explanation; she was familiar with shiatsu. "Stress is a main underlying cause of what troubles most of these women, coupled with poor nutrition," she said. "Why don't you try some shiatsu on them right now?"

I never would have been so bold as to make that suggestion myself, but I was thrilled when she did. She instructed Massoud to bring in a long, flat cushion. He initially objected, fearing the women might soil the cushion with menstrual blood, but Dr. Roshanak insisted. We placed it on the floor and she began summoning the women. One or two came in at a time. They pulled off their burqas, revealing dresses made of thin and worn material. Dr. Roshanak talked to each one for a few minutes, scolding some. "She keeps having too many babies," Dr. Roshanak complained to me of one woman who stood before her. "Show how many times you've become pregnant," she instructed the woman in Pashto. The woman obediently raised nine fingers, eliciting a frustrated sigh from Dr. Roshanak. "I'm trying to teach her how to tell her husband no." Even I, though, knew that was a lesson unlikely to hold.

Then Dr. Roshanak handed over pills, listened to their hearts, probed their abdomens. When her examination was finished, she told each patient to lie down on the mat and urged me to go to work.

How can I describe what it was like to give these women shiatsu? It is unlikely that any of them had ever seen an American woman in person before, and I am sure none had ever been touched by one, or even received any kind of massage. I was blond, spoke a different language, probably even smelled alien, and was trying to connect to them in an unfamiliar way with an objective wholly unknown to them. I simply wanted to help them relax and let go. I doubt anyone had ever suggested that to them before. On top of that, I couldn't make my suggestion with words.

I'd been trained to start a shiatsu session by kneeling on the floor, resting my hands on the belly, or the *hara,* and breathing for several minutes in concert with my client. But I sensed putting my hands immediately on these women's abdomens might feel too intimate to them, so I often started with a quick squeeze of their fingers, as if to communicate my good intentions, and then had them lie on their stomachs. I stroked down the center of their backs several times, practiced *ken beki,* a gentle rocking motion on the lower back, massaged their waists, and then leaned into the points along their bladder meridian, which flows next to the spine. I sat by their heads and worked in similar ways on their necks and shoulders. Sometimes I worked the pressure points in their hands or feet, or had them turn over so I could massage their scalps, foreheads, and temples. I kept each session short, fifteen minutes at most.

"They could get used to this, I'm sure, and so could I. Why don't you stay and work with me?" Dr. Roshanak asked, only half kidding. Fully illogical because of familial and professional obligations, her offer was nevertheless tempting. I felt briefly connected to these Afghan women on an intimately physical level, and that seemed to me at the moment to be more intrinsically human than the more traditional types of exchanges between war-battered Afghans and American soldiers or aid workers.

My awareness grew sharper as I knelt and practiced shiatsu on the floor in Massoud's home, a breeze stirring the window's light curtain, the scent of cooking rice in the air. I became ultraconscious of my weight as I leaned into them, and I didn't want my touch to feel invasive or uncomfortable. They were, each one, far thinner than they looked under those flowing burqas. My thumbs sank deeply into their ribs, and I dared not use my elbows. Their muscles felt stringy to my hands, their bones brittle.

I wanted the women to be at ease, and that was a challenge. Of the dozen or so I worked on, only one seemed to truly relax. She sprawled out, a sense of complete confidence emanating from her body. The contrast between her and the others was so marked that I almost giggled, and I never could fathom what triggered that absolute trust. Generally, the women were polite but cautious when Dr. Roshanak instructed them to lie down. "Breathe," she would occasionally command, and that would result in one or two heavy, tense inhalations.

But after each session, before shrugging their burqas back on, the women—some grandmothers, others hardly out of their teens—gave me hugs. Some of them laughed or touched my cheek before parting. It was as though something unnameable had been sealed between us.

The sessions continued until Massoud came and banged on the door. "Masha. Roshanak. Come eat lunch," he called, his voice insistent. "Now." He returned five minutes later, calling for us again.

"You go," Dr. Roshanak said. "It will make him more patient. I will be there in a few minutes." Though I wasn't ready to stop, Dr. Roshanak, I knew, was not a woman with whom to argue.

* * *

That evening, as Massoud drove me back to the small guesthouse where I was staying in Kabul, I began thinking about their bodies, mine, ours. What is a woman's body? To a man, it is often a thing of poetry—a blossom, a narrowing and then a widening, a luscious curve. And because men poeticize our bodies, we may tend to look at them, too, through the eyes of someone else. Being serviceable is suddenly not enough. We long for more: cantaloupe breasts, sculpted abs, legs longer than night itself. We go to extraordinary lengths to remake ourselves in an image of beauty.

But none of the Afghan women to whom I'd just had the privilege of giving shiatsu had ever heard of a spa or a personal trainer, plastic surgery or control-top stockings. Or, for that matter, a shelter for battered women. Their bodies were underfed, overworked, and barely considered their own. As I knelt and stroked their backs or squeezed their necks or used my thumbs to rub circles on their scalps, I understood that our Western preoccupation with our physical flaws is, in fact, a luxury. In Afghanistan, even the little celebrations of the body—a shoulder rub, a dive into a pool of water, or a balm to rub into knees and elbows—are a rare if not impossible extravagance.

It's been two years since that visit. The stunningly brave Dr. Roshanak went on to win a parliament seat, though her home was attacked by automatic weapons and rockets during the campaign. She continues to see far-flung patients in her cousin's house, despite her added responsibilities. Burqas remain commonplace, lotion is still a luxury, and "vice and virtue" police are reappearing on Kabul's streets to insist that women keep their bodies covered. As for me, I remain deeply linked to and inspired by those women in ways that are difficult to express or even fully explain. I learned much in Afghanistan. But the most significant lesson may have been the importance of touch in connecting people from unimaginably different lives and circumstances and allowing them to communicate in a place that exists beyond mere words.

Betrayed

Victoria Zackheim

Compton was a mean little city. Invisible grids separated the races, black and white never merging. From kindergarten through high school graduation, in a Los Angeles suburb fast becoming predominately African American, the only black student in my school was a girl in the special program for the deaf. A good number of my classmates were smug about living on the right side of town—which meant east of the railroad tracks—but where I lived and who I was felt terribly, terribly wrong.

My parents were red-diaper babies—children born of left-wingers, primarily Jews from Eastern Europe—who became deeply involved in civil rights in a town where there were few. And, to add more fertilizer to the ingredients comprising this childhood bomb, my father was an educator on the other side of the tracks. By the age of seven, I was accustomed to being called "dirty Jew" by neighborhood children. By ten, when my father became principal of a middle school in West Compton, I began to hear "nigger-lover" from fellow students and a few of my teachers. But when my father became principal of the only all-black high school in town, a school that not only beat us at every sport but also sent more students on to higher education than Compton's two other high schools combined, the epithet was cranked up to "nigger-loving Jew." I can still see those deep bruises on my arm, inflicted by a history teacher who doubled as a coach. To a child in the bitter trials of adolescence, these epithets and bruises were strung out like a mysterious mathematical equation adding up to isolation and misery and a sense of never fitting in while desperately yearning to belong.

The verbal attacks I suffered, while being told by my parents that I had to stand up to those attacks—after all, we were right, they were wrong (but try explaining that to a child whose teachers are pulling her aside and demanding to know what in the hell her father thinks he's doing, *trying to educate those damn niggers*)—should have felt like the worst sort of betrayal. But it wasn't. That was reserved for what happened shortly after I turned ten: I began to menstruate, and I was so utterly unprepared for what was considered my introduction to womanhood that even today I sometimes wonder if I have recovered from the shock.

Ten years old. Sanitary napkins were designed for mature bodies. Those bulky, coarse pads chafed my inner thighs until the skin was raw. The ends of the pads were anchored to cruel metal hooks attached to a wide elastic belt that held the thing in place. With my little-girl-round belly, the belt often rolled itself into a rope that cut into my stomach and slipped down my hips. We wore skirts then, no slacks, and I lived in horror of standing up in my fifth-grade class and having the entire contraption drop to the floor. (And could a child of ten understand that she needed to pull it all down before using the toilet? Evidently not, because on that first day, we visited family friends for a barbeque and I stood alone in the bathroom, trying to reason through the process. I cannot recall why, but I somehow determined that I should leave everything in place while I peed. When I returned to the patio and sat down, there was a dramatic *squish* and moments later we were in the car, I was sitting on a borrowed towel—surely there must have been a way for my mother to borrow the damned thing without having to explain why!—and my older sister was doing a very poor job of keeping a hand clamped over her mouth to quell the laughter.)

Plummeting pads and the logistics of hygiene were a small part of the nightmare. I could have endured the discomfort of the apparatus and the confusion wrought by ovaries insisting I abandon childhood and enter the age of reproduction. I could have endured as well the humiliation of changing my pad in the girls' bathroom of Theodore Roosevelt Elementary School while classmates— most of whom were to wait several years before facing this dramatic event—stood upon toilet seats in the adjoining stalls to peer over, fascinated to see a little girl struggling with something their mothers did behind locked doors.

What I could not endure, however, was the message that I was no longer to be left alone with the sons of my parents' friends. Wherever that boy and I happened to be visiting, the door remained open. If we were in a bedroom, we were to sit on the floor, never the bed. I felt confused and humiliated whenever my mother poked her head into the room and chirped, "Just checking!" Just checking what? That her bewildered little girl wasn't getting it on with some ten-year-old boy?

I can't recall the actual words, but I do remember the subtleties of body language and facial expressions alerting me to the dangers of having been thrust into, and perhaps being only inches away from falling victim to, that dangerous and tempting world of groping, hot sex. But I was only ten. What the hell was sex?

I loved to ride my bicycle around the neighborhood, sailing along Holly Street on my sky-blue Schwinn, with playing cards attached to its frame by a wooden clothespin giving off wonderful *flap-flap* sounds as the wheels rotated. With the arrival of "the curse" (a.k.a. "the guest," "the visitor," "the little friend"), my bike was soon relegated to the garage. Even though it was only one week each month, the trauma of pumping the pedals while perched on an inch of lumpy cotton, metal points inflicting stigmata, cheated me of the joy of flight I had once known.

At the age of ten, I was into Carolyn Keene mysteries and Puccini operas. I was a clever child, so my parents assumed I was absorbing data, their subtle comments on sexuality and procreation, and storing that information in my clever little brain. In the same way I turned off my auditory receptors whenever my parents spoke Yiddish—if they wanted me to understand, wouldn't they say it in English?—so, too, did I manage to shut out comments and clues relating to the human body, especially mine.

It wasn't long before I recognized how my parents' behavior toward me changed, how I began to feel as if I had done something wrong. There was sudden attention to what I wore. With my breasts getting larger and my waist tapering, scoop-neck shirts and little-girl shorts were replaced by modest blouses and pedal pushers. Oh yes, and cotton brassieres.

We were a family of four: my parents, my older sister, and me. Our home was two small bedrooms, a bathroom, a cozy living room, and kitchen. There was little space for privacy, yet we managed to create air around ourselves. What my parents could not have foretold was how this fierce modesty informed me not only that it was shameful to see a man's body, but that it was even more shameful for a man to see mine.

After I began to menstruate, my mother became severely protective and my father inexplicably took his distance. One of my greatest joys had been to climb onto his lap and have a good visit. Suddenly, Daddy was happy to chat, but the physical intimacy had ended. The closest I could manage was to sit next to him while we shared the pleasure of the *Saturday Review* double acrostic puzzle. I yearned to reclaim that place on his lap, signifying my place as the baby of the family, but a few days of bleeding each month had made me a pariah . . . who happened to be ten years old.

By age twelve, I learned to recognize a certain look on a man's face. I saw it in the fathers of playmates, in their older brothers and their friends, how their eyes moved slowly across my chest, how their nostrils flared and their expressions became intense, purposeful. By thirteen, I knew to fold my arms so that those breasts were covered.

Nothing had prepared me for school dances, for the horror of being held close by pubescent boys who, while attempting to grind an insubstantial penis against me, perspired profusely and left rank odors on my skin and clothing. Nor was I prepared for their rushing past me in the hallway, suddenly reaching out and grabbing my breasts. And if this were not sufficiently traumatizing, they bragged to one another, boasting about their conquest as if I had been somehow complicit. In what was a pre-backpack society, I learned to walk with binder and textbooks clutched against me, armor shielding my maidenhood from scandal.

It was around this time that an obstruction began to form between thought and feeling, a barrier interfering with the merging of senses. It would be years, decades, before I learned to recognize its presence and address it.

My mother became ill when I entered my teenage years, and my family's primary focus was her survival. In time, her health deteriorated until she was near death. Our little house made it impossible to escape the rhythmic, oxygen-pumping hiss of the Bennett machine that she used whenever her breathing was labored. I hated the sound of that behemoth lifesaver, but its prolonged silence was even worse, because this indicated that she was hospitalized.

My daily schedule became as predictable as her hospitalizations: go to school, rush home to see if Mom were still alive, close myself in my room and refuse to come out, do everything teenage-possible to not be a loving, nurturing daughter. Between school, hospital visits, the never-ending racist comments directed at me by students (out of utter cruelty) and by teachers (out of resentment and small-minded ideals), and living in an inexorable state of fear about being left motherless (and secretly wishing that my mother would just die and get it over with), I managed to stumble through adolescence without learning anything more about sex than I knew at age ten. Despite my sister's attempts to care for me and act the parent to this bewildered child, and despite my parents' attempts to direct some attention my way, I quietly slipped into an abyss of insecurity and self-loathing.

By fifteen, I believed that I had managed to create a safety zone in a hostile world. I knew to slouch over my enormous breasts, to dress in baggy, ill-fitting clothing, and to keep vivid and frequent suicidal fantasies to myself. I gained weight because it made sense that a fat girl would be spared leering suggestions made by men the age of her father. I snubbed the role of the coquette, leaving it to classmates who understood such mysteries as sleeping with rollers in their hair, applying makeup, and giggling cutely when passing a boy in the hall. If a boy showed any interest in me, my radar went haywire. Part of me was pleased, yet I was agonizingly shy. It was a shyness I learned to conceal behind a quick wit and sometimes scathing humor. I soon discovered that, even while backing away from male attention, the ghost of my mother—not dead, just persistent—hovered nearby. "Boys just want one thing," came her warning. So, while my chastity made the vestal virgins seem downright slutty by comparison, I dealt with the fear that I was viewed as the class whore.

High school classmates dropped out, some leaving town to live with an aunt in Iowa or attend a special school in Tennessee. "She's pregnant," my mother would insist. I argued bitterly with her, my innocence so absolute that I truly believed that no one I knew would stoop to engage in s-e-x. Even when my mother was proven right, I could not concede.

At seventeen, it was time to leave home. I was feverish with the thrill of getting out of town and beginning a new life at university. I was packed, ready to drag clothing and bedding out to the car, when my mother, the same woman who had questioned my morals for years, took me by the shoulders, smiled sweetly, and said, "Remember, darling, just because you sleep with a man doesn't mean you have to marry him."

As a freshman at UCLA, I lived in a coed dorm and had more dates during that first month on campus than in my last two years of high school. Some of the boys were in fact men, seniors, veterans in the game of sex, who assumed that big breasts promised an easy conquest. So off I went to fraternity parties (He asked me! *Me!*) and watched couples disappear into rooms, heard laughter behind closed doors, yet had little inkling that I was expected to play that game. That is, until The Party. The rum punch made me sick. Would I like to lie down in the pledge dorm until I felt better? Oh yes, thank you very much. And then the rules of the game were explained forcefully: A football linebacker, two hundred and sixty-five convincing pounds, mercifully too drunk to hold down (much less penetrate) a girl half his weight who was prepared to fight to the death before losing her precious virginity to some semiliterate thug.

After months of weekend nights of being escorted to the dorm elevator and noticing how all those boys (including my dates) covered wet spots on their pants, I reasoned it out and came up with the logical answer: Heavy kissing made boys urinate.

I wanted to belong, to be considered exciting and beautiful, and a steady stream of boys and men apparently found me so. I recall being horror-struck when a charming and married professor of Italian drove me home from class in his hot little sports car and ran his hand up my leg. (Looking back, I do have regrets about turning him down, and that little incident continues to provide some lively sexual fantasies forty-five years later.) But I was so young, and putting out was not something I intended to do. So I fended off the tempting offers and forced a smile when "uptight" and "ice queen" were tossed my way. (And, to be frank, I much preferred "ice queen" to "nigger-loving Jew.")

I played it safe, married a sweet fellow student who shared my innocence, got the sex thing handled, or so I thought. My weight went up and down, depending on how I was feeling about my role as woman, wife, mother. My body functioned but I was unaware of its presence, that barrier having become a well-formed metal hatch that separated torso from brain, compressing all emotions below while allowing the intellect to take over and provide what I assumed were logical explanations for my feelings. Sexual stirrings were terrifying, out-of-control feelings that caused me to shut down even more. I quickly mastered the art of denying the presence of emotions entirely until, in time, this psychological void became physical and I no longer felt at all. Numb mind, numb body. Sex was not for pleasure but for satisfying a marriage contract.

Frigidity, anger, self-hatred. I was suddenly thirty-five and viewed my life as a stagnant, slow-moving river with no rapids, no bends and curves, nothing to stop the flow from moving endlessly toward an infinite body of water where either I would be lost forever or, if luck were on my side, I would drown. And then divorce, grief, such a profound sense of grief and failure that I began to understand that I must either loosen that hatch or squander the chance to feel alive. I remember sitting in the therapist's office, afternoon light streaming into the room and illuminating dust particles. I could have watched that light for an hour—and would have, had the soft-spoken woman not insisted that I communicate. "What are you feeling?" she asked, and a very large accumulation of self-hatred welled up, threatening to cut off my oxygen. It was a triumphant moment in my quest for mental health when I could finally look her in the eye and say, "I feel fuck-all nothing. Nothing."

When my younger child left for college, I lived alone for the first time in my life. Nested into my wonderful 1905 Craftsman-like bungalow near the Stanford campus, I reveled in the quiet, in the opportunity to look back at the mother I had been (not great) and the opportunities that lay ahead to be a better mother (which I think I became). But soon, into that thrilling silence, arrived a voice, one I had managed to avoid for nearly forty years. It informed me that I was a fraud, a woman who performed with smiles and laughter but whose heart was locked down, whose self-loathing was profound. Perhaps this was the price for ignoring that rusted hatch, for being a young divorced woman with too many lovers and too few loves. How could I pry open that damned hatch if I lacked the proper tools? And when would I finally feel good about myself? Perhaps I deserved that glare from my daughter or that angry remark from my son, the desirable man who didn't ask me out or the undesirable man who did. As confused as I was, as wretched as I felt, I was still able to care enough for myself to understand that a dramatic change was required. Without it, I might not survive.

With both children off to university, I sold my home, took my computer and six cartons of clothing, books, and assorted mementos, and left for a three-month stay in Paris, where it was my intention to (a) study French and (b) find myself. (In those days, we were always trying to find ourselves, my generation believing that the self was somehow lost and in need of being found.) Living far from my safety net, I began to explore ways to separate from the woman I had been throughout my adult life. The process was as exhilarating as it was devastatingly lonely.

The three months became a year, and then two, and then nearly five. There were a few lovers and many long, soul-searching walks. There were also caring French friends who generously pulled me into their lives and shared a cultural richness I had been longing to taste. It was there, isolated from my entire history, that I discovered in myself an untapped daring, the courage to go it alone, and the muscle required to scrape and pry, oil and jimmy, until that hatch began to budge. It took five years of geographic isolation before I was reminded what I had known as a little girl before menstruation, before significant breasts and the attention of inattentive men: that I could love myself; that I could experience perfect joy; that I could be alone and not be lonely, reveling in my own good company. I began to see how those countless protective layers created during a lifetime could be removed, painstakingly, one by one, along with the bolts securing that hatch. I also learned that I no longer had to suppress those emotions I once feared would rise up and suffocate me or be fearful that high school classmates or imagined goblins from my past would slither out and threaten my existence.

At sixty-two, I carry too much weight, have occasional visions of full-body liposuction, and often wish with heartbreaking sincerity that I could go back thirty years and do it better: avoid those fats, run those miles, be a better mother, moisturize. Despite my neglect, my body has been good to me. Being healthy, I'm able to live life as I choose. I have dear friends, a family that loves me, and an occasional man. As for the hatch: It exists, sometimes threatens, but mainly it's my reminder of how quickly I can shut down. What matters is that I no longer fear it. The right tools, a can of oil, and a user's manual remain safely within reach.

The Teardrop

Rochelle Jewel Shapiro

I always prided myself on being robust and hardy like my Russian grandmother, my Bubbie. I inherited not only her psychic gift but also her sturdy body and physical endurance. With her husband already in America, Bubbie had to carry her youngest child on her back, and all their possessions, in order to lead her four older children out of their burning village, where the Cossacks were waging another pogrom. And in America, not only was she a healer with a blockful of customers waiting on her doorstep, but she cooked for the whole family, nursed everyone who got sick, and kept at it well into her eighties.

My husband, Bernie, also worked such long hours that he might as well have been in a different country. While he worked at his pharmacy, I mowed the steep hill of our lawn and shoveled the deep snow from our long driveway, all with my toddler, Charles, in a carrier on my back and Heather, three years older, hanging on to my skirt. Bernie was proud that I could raise two small children and manage the house, plus earn money as a phone psychic. But one day, I woke up with tight muscles. *Nothing,* I told myself. I had been doing spring-cleaning the day before, hauling bags of things we didn't need to the charity drop box in town. But my muscles remained tight, no matter how much Bengay I used or how much I rested. As time went on, I was constantly spraining something and hobbling about with an Ace bandage wrapped around a limb. My eyes, tongue, throat, and the inside of my nose began to burn. I got pounding headaches and was tired all the time; if someone sneezed in my presence, I caught a cold that I couldn't shake without antibiotics. My internist checked me out thoroughly and gave me blood tests. The tests came back normal.

"You're perfectly healthy," he said.

But I knew I was sick. I left his office determined to find out what was wrong. I went home and lit a lavender-scented candle. (Bubbie had always puffed lavender talc on her neck.) I closed my eyes and, with each exhale, chanted *om.* I imagined my body as the plastic anatomy model that my fourth-grade teacher had kept on her desk, with organs, blood vessels, bones, and muscles illuminated. I looked for dark spots, as I did for my clients. I was always sending them to a doctor if I saw a shadow on a breast or a dark spot on a lung. But now I didn't see any dark spots. "Bubbie," I called out. "I need your help."

I waited for a glimpse of her with those pale eyes, high cheekbones, and white hair braided and coiled on top of her head like a crown; for a warmth or tingling in my arm, as if she were brushing against me. I listened hard for a word whispered in her Yiddish accent, but there was no sign of her presence. I felt disappointed, abandoned, and then I saw the outline of a teardrop coming from nowhere. Did it mean I was feeling too sorry for myself? Maybe the doctor was right. Maybe I was perfectly healthy.

Downstairs, my children called out, "Mommy, we want a magic carpet ride."

I went down and unfolded the old quilt and ceremoniously flapped it in the air three times, and then I set it down on the floor before them. I always pulled them around the polished-wood living room floor as I *whooshed* like the wind. Giggling, they sat in the middle of the blanket and held on to each other. I gripped two corners and pulled, but for the first time, nothing happened.

"Mommy, stop fooling around," Heather said, disappointed.

I was astonished. I gripped the blanket with both hands and pulled as hard as I could, tipping back to give myself leverage, but again, nothing.

"What's the matter, Mommy?" Heather asked, a little crease of worry appearing between her small eyebrows.

I felt my face trembling as I tried to keep from crying. "I guess I'm just a little tired," I said.

"Magic carpet ride!" Charles bawled.

Heather, still eyeing me with concern, hollered, "Shut up, baby!" and bopped him on his curly blond head.

The following day I made an appointment with a doctor who, according to *New York* magazine, was one of the best in the city. He examined me thoroughly, ran tests, and at my next appointment announced, "Your health is excellent."

"But I'm too weak to pull my children on a blanket," I protested.

He rolled his eyes. "There's nothing in my examination or the bloodwork that would substantiate that," he insisted, and then he looked at his watch.

When I complained to Bernie, he told me to go to a doctor who he had heard was a great diagnostician.

As the doctor put the stethoscope to my chest, he got a call. "Excuse me," he said. "I've got to take this; it's my lawyer. I'm in the middle of a bitter divorce. My wife is after every penny I ever earned." Then, instead of calling me with the test results, he phoned Bernie.

"Dr. Farkis called today," Bernie said. "I thought he wanted to check on a patient's prescription, but he told me, 'Your wife is a hypochondriac. Don't let her get away with it. Next thing you know, she'll claim she can't work anymore and you'll have to give her a huge divorce settlement.'"

I thrust out my chin. "You must have really told him off," I said.

"Well, this is the third doctor who's found nothing wrong," Bernie said. "Maybe it *is* something emotional."

"Don't you believe I'm not feeling well?" I asked, stung.

"I believe that you believe it," he said.

Bernie's doubts hung in the house and began to seep into me. Maybe I was making up the symptoms. The next time I felt too tired to move, I said to myself, *Faker*, and forced myself to get into the car and drive to the supermarket. On the way, the car in front of me stopped short and I was so drowsy that I crashed into it.

I tried to build my strength with exercise. Instead of getting stronger, I got inflammation in my knees and elbows. It was so hard for me to get my son to the playground every day that I enrolled him in an all-day nursery program.

"I just took out a loan because Medicaid and the HMOs have delayed their payments again," Bernie said that night. "We're barely paying our mortgage and now we have tuition for a two-year-old!"

I felt like a boulder chained to his ankle; I didn't know what to do, where to go. I sat in meditation again, but all I saw was the same teardrop. Maybe I was getting to be like an aunt on my mother's side, who always suffered from oddball ailments, wearing wool socks to bed even in summertime. That was enough to make me decide to go to a psychiatrist. But I didn't want to tell Bernie. It would have been like admitting that I was making up the symptoms.

Dr. Price's office was in the rear of his house, and the dog barked as I passed the window. I sat on his leather couch and he asked me about my childhood. After I told him at length about my father, mother, two sisters, and little brother, I said, "The doctors and my husband are accusing me of being a hypochondriac, but my symptoms are very real. Can I tell you what they are?"

"No," he said. "When your baby brother was born, how did you feel about him having a penis?" I laughed out loud, the first good laugh I'd had since I'd begun to feel sick. One of his eyebrows shot up. "Next week at eleven, then. . . ." he said.

I stood up. "I'll call you," I said. I never did.

My problems were mounting. Not only was I not pulling my weight at home, but whatever was wrong seemed to be spreading to my gums, which had always been fine. Our insurance didn't cover my periodontal surgeries. The financial strain was too much for Bernie. He came home more and more stressed. When he walked through the door, he no longer smiled at me.

"You don't even talk to me anymore," I said on one of the rare nights he was home early.

He raised one hand wearily. "I just need a quiet dinner," he said.

The kids were kicking each other under the table and I picked at my food.

"You're not going to eat?" he asked me.

"My gums are still swollen from the surgery," I said.

"Your dentist is bleeding this family dry!" he said, standing up so suddenly that his chair tipped back and clattered to the floor.

The children put down their spoons and stared at him, then at me.

I bit my lip so I wouldn't say anything to escalate the situation. My body was suffering and so was my marriage.

In desperation, I did research on holistic health centers and found one run by two doctors who employed the techniques of the famous psychic Edgar Cayce. One night I showed the brochure to Bernie. "Our insurance wouldn't cover this," he said, his face twitching with anger. "You went to doctor after doctor and they all said the same thing: It's all in your head."

"You don't understand," I said. "I'm getting headaches, sprains, my eyes and nose burn, I'm tired all the time, and my throat is raw. I feel like I'm a hundred years old."

Even though I knew that going to this healing center would put our marriage at greater risk, I enlisted the help of my sister to pitch in, hired sitters, and flew to Arizona. At the center I found out that the treatment for each patient was the same, no matter what the ailment was: hot castor-oil packs applied to the liver and various other organs; hot steam baths; drops of castor oil taken in water; a mostly vegetarian diet; hard massage; and healing visualizations. "How could every patient get the same treatment?" I asked the holistic doctor.

"Every illness has the same origin—disease," he explained.

I had doubts, but it seemed that my marriage was going to be over any minute if I didn't get well. "I have so many symptoms that I'm not sure what to visualize," I said, and I told him what they were.

"Just visualize yourself smiling and happy," he advised.

After a couple of weeks of heat treatments and massage, my skin became raw and painful, and I was oversensitive to heat and cold. Even at room temperature, my skin burned.

"You're just releasing toxins," the new-age doctor told me. "Stay with the treatments and you'll be well in no time."

All around me other patients were improving dramatically. A man I had chatted with held two x-rays up to the light. "See the tumor I had on my leg?" he said. "Big as a plum.

It's on a nerve and the doctors couldn't promise I'd be able to walk. Look at my latest picture," he boasted, and I was amazed to see that the plum had shriveled to raisin size.

An elderly man whose arm had been paralyzed by a stroke showed me how he could now move his fingers. A middle-aged woman who had been covered with psoriasis pulled her sweater off her shoulder to flaunt her clear skin.

I stayed at the center for ten days, and then went home and continued the hot castor-oil packs and steam showers. I also went to someone who gave the same hard massage I'd had at the clinic. The doctor had promised that I'd see results in three months, but what I saw were hands that looked like pink blown-up latex gloves. My nose, lips, earlobes, and eyelids were swollen, too. "I'm worse," I had to admit to Bernie.

"You had to go to Hypochondriacs' Heaven and waste even more money," he said, his face dark. We didn't speak for the rest of the day.

The next day he said, so quietly that I had to lean toward him, "The apartment over the store is empty now. I'll take the kids out on weekends. With the hours I work, they don't even have to know that I moved out." As he packed his bags, I saw tears in his eyes, but still he left.

The snow fell the following Monday, and when Heather looked out the window she cried in alarm, "Daddy didn't leave footprints."

A month later I got the flu, with a high fever and a terrible cough. I certainly didn't want to go to the doctor who told Bernie I was a hypochondriac, so I picked one from our insurance list and decided not to tell him about my other symptoms. When I got there, I said matter-of-factly, "I have the flu," as if I were a normal person.

He took a long look at my throat, lifted my tongue, and looked all around my mouth. He held up my eyelids and looked into my eyes. "Have your eyes been bothering you?" he asked.

"Yes," I admitted.

"Does your throat hurt even when you don't have the flu?"

I nodded.

"What about aches and pains? Headaches? Fatigue?"

I nodded again.

"I'm taking some bloodwork," he told me.

I left feeling a little more hopeful. I told myself that I didn't care what he found or how horrible it was, as long as he didn't say there was nothing wrong with me.

I tried not to think about Bernie. On weekends, when he came to pick up the children, I made sure to stay upstairs with the blinds closed. I had to focus on myself and getting better.

A couple of weeks later, the nurse called to tell me that the doctor wanted me to come in and discuss my test results. I sat in his office, twisting the strap of my handbag. I couldn't read his expression.

"You have Sjögren's syndrome," he told me.

Finally, a name for all the misery I was going through. "What's that?" I asked, leaning forward in my chair.

"An autoimmune disorder, a little-known sister of lupus. It's a form of arthritis that attacks the glands." He rattled off a few of the illnesses that could arise from this one. "Sarcoma, melanoma, lymphoma, strokes, kidney failure, a mouth so dry that one's voice becomes a rusty hinge, eye maladies from the dryness, bowel troubles, gerd—that's reflux—and periodontal disease."

My heart beat faster. "I went to so many doctors, and they told me I was imagining all the symptoms."

He looked delighted with himself.

"So what do I do to get well?"

"There's no cure," he said, and I felt my delight leaving. "And because Sjögren's affects the blood vessels," he went on, "you should never have had all those treatments in Arizona. That quackery has done permanent damage to your circulation."

I started to cry, but, because of the dryness, no tears would come.

"Those muscle aches might be from fibromyalgia," he said, "but I'll have to check your trigger points to be sure."

"Is there any cure for fibromyalgia?" I asked.

He shook his head.

"Never mind, then," I said. "Sjögren's is more than enough."

The doctor continued speaking, but I didn't hear anything else because my heart was drumming in my ears.

"I'll see you in three months," he said, but I didn't stop at the receptionist's desk for an appointment. I couldn't bear to hear any more bad news about my body. I continued walking, got in my car, and drove straight to Bernie's pharmacy. He was behind the prescription counter, and I could hear the *ping* of pills dropping onto the round plate. There were customers waiting, but I went straight behind the counter.

He looked up, his eyes widening in surprise.

"You were wrong, all wrong," I blurted. "I *am* sick. Really sick." I felt the customers' eyes on me, so I lowered my voice. "I have Sjögren's syndrome," I said, and I repeated what the doctor had said, even about the harm done by the holistic treatments. I didn't want to hold anything back. "I would never have gone to that clinic if you had believed me. You made me feel worthless."

He was silent, and then he cupped my face in his hands. "God, I'm so sorry," he said. "So very sorry."

"Doc, I need my prescription," a customer called out, but Bernie didn't answer. He just kept looking into my face. "You need me and I'm coming home," he said.

"No," I said. "I've managed fine without you."

"Then I need you and I'm coming home," he said.

Unlike Bubbie, I would never be able to carry my child on my back while hauling featherbeds and brass candlesticks and bags of potatoes through the forest to get away from the Cossacks and their snarling dogs. But then, living in Great Neck, Long Island, there would be no need for that. I could no longer roughhouse with my kids or give them magic carpet rides. But I could still read them stories and doodle with them and listen to their breathless voices as they told me about the class bully or which kid was sent to the time-out corner. And I could teach them how to tell time and how to write down their thoughts in diaries that, as grownups, they still treasure. I couldn't play tennis with my husband or go golfing, like other women on the block, but on days when I felt well enough, we could walk through the botanical gardens, our fingers entwined, or go to the movies, our heads on each other's shoulders. And my psychic gift was still intact, so I could continue being of service to my clients.

I signed up for the self-help newsletter for Sjögren's syndrome. When it came in the mail, I sucked in my breath: The logo was a single teardrop, like the one I had seen when I tried to diagnose myself.

If only I had trusted my body more and been patient with my suffering, maybe the meaning of that teardrop would have revealed itself and I would have been healthier than I am today. But I had felt abandoned and was unable to see how Bubbie had sent me that teardrop as the answer. Instead of accepting illness gracefully, I turned it against myself as a sign of my weakness and self-pity. I thought my body had betrayed me; by not listening to its messages, I had betrayed it.

It isn't easy being chronically ill, but I've promised to love my body every day, no matter how much it's hurting. Now I wrap my arms around myself, and in the mirror I see my eyes, anointed with artificial tears, shine with joy.

The Best Birthday of All

Barbara Abercrombie

My sixtieth birthday was the best birthday of my life. Better than turning eighteen or twenty-one, even better than childhood birthdays. I would like to say that this was because of my great strength of character and hard-won knowledge, or some other attribute that I had single-handedly wrestled from life, something that I could pass on to you, but the fact is, it was luck.

I was alive. I was loved.

But maybe luck in itself can be inspiring. And maybe it's important to remember how unexpectedly luck can come along at a dark time, and to realize that when it does, luck needs to be recognized and invited in, held on to.

My fortieth birthday had been dreadful: My husband and I had a huge fight over whether I should stop work on my novel that day so I could take his car in for an oil change. My fiftieth was even worse: Our marriage had begun its final downward spiral. I was depressed, I was fifty years old. My husband was depressed: He was married to a fifty-year-old woman. A year later, he had an affair with a younger woman and I left him. It was one of those times in life when you figure if you can just keep breathing, you're doing okay. My father had died a few months before, my mother was ill with heart disease, and both my cats had died that summer. I kept breathing. For the first time in my life, I couldn't read for solace; I couldn't concentrate. Even teaching, I couldn't plan and organize in advance; I'd just wing it. I was fifty-one years old and felt more ancient than the pyramids.

One of my best male friends, R, had recently been divorced and he took me out to dinner a lot. I couldn't get to the entrée without bursting into tears and having to borrow a handkerchief from him. (This was the kind of man who carried pure white handkerchiefs.) For six months I couldn't get through dinner without weeping, and by then I had a stash of his pure white handkerchiefs. About a year later, he asked me to marry him. "I'm never getting married again," I told him, absolutely convinced of what I was saying. I would never, ever hand over my life, my heart, to another man. I was starting to pull myself together; I'd bought a house; I could support myself; I was learning to live alone. But I thanked R for asking. He went off and dated other women while my husband and I tried to repair our marriage, but whatever we were doing, R and I ended up calling each other and talking about it.

Six years later, in a hotel room in London, after much drama, therapy, and reflection on my part, R again asked me to marry him and I said yes.

We decided to get married the following summer and have a real wedding. When we announced our engagement to our five children (who had grown up with each other), they were happy with our news. It was as if life had *burst* into happiness. I loved this man; he'd been my friend for all these years; we never ran out of anything to talk about; we jumped into bed at every opportunity. I felt like a teenager. But it was so much better than being a teenager! In my teens, I was always deep into angst and worried about my hair.

In February, we set our wedding date for August fifteenth. February was the month I usually had my yearly mammogram, which I'd forgotten about in the excitement of our engagement. When I called for an appointment, I couldn't get one until a few months later, which was just fine, because I was busy working and trying to plan the wedding, and since I was a vegetarian, a runner, and hadn't smoked for twenty years, I really wasn't too worried about having breast cancer. To be responsible, though, I checked my breasts one morning in bed. I found nothing unusual, but, realizing it had been actually longer than a year since my last mammogram, I asked R to check them too.

"Here's something," he said. I felt where he pointed, and yes, there was the tiniest lump, a little pea of a lump next to my left nipple. "Well, it takes an engineer to find these things," I said. He's an engineer, it was a joke, but he didn't think I was funny. "Call and move up your appointment," he said. So I did, and an available appointment miraculously appeared when I said the magic words "lump in my breast." Then we went off to Palm Springs for the weekend and made love a lot and I didn't think about the lump at all until my appointment Monday morning.

In the waiting room, surrounded by other women, it was oddly peaceful and pleasant. The walls were painted lavender, sunlight spilled through the open windows, and the air smelled of grass being mowed. A Muzak version of "People Will Say We're in Love" played. A woman in her late seventies, sitting across from me with two friends, hummed along. A younger woman sitting next to me, wearing a scarf that covered her bald head, wrote Valentine's cards.

I knew the drill: no perfume or deodorant, sweater and bra off, johnny gown on and open in the front, my breast kneaded into position and then flattened rather alarmingly under a transparent vise. "Hold your breath!" the technician sang out from the safety of her fortified bunker. I held my breath as the machine whirred.

When she finished, I pointed out the lump next to my left nipple. I was expecting a shrug, maybe recognition of my possible hypochondria, even though this tiny lump that R had found was absolutely nothing. Instead, the technician's face was serious as she felt it. Then she put a tag on the lump, kind of a breast Post-it, and scheduled me for an immediate ultrasound.

I wanted to tell her that I was getting married in six months, that I taught two courses and had a lot of students, I was writing a novel, and I didn't have time for this. But I waited, and I did have the exam. And then a doctor I had never met before told me I needed to see a breast surgeon right away to have the lump surgically removed and biopsied.

The morning of the biopsy, R and I had a long-standing appointment with the priest who was going to marry us. We reserved the chapel for the evening of August fifteenth and discussed our vows with him, the music we wanted, and my idea of lighting the chapel with candles and filling it with white flowers. I didn't mention to the priest that our next stop that day was the hospital; I felt like I was living in alternative universes.

I'm not very religious, but I love the ritual and music and language of my church. Would prayers do any good? I wondered. R and I went into the chapel before we headed to the hospital. I really didn't believe that if this lump were cancer, God would suddenly melt it away for me. But I did get down on my knees in a pew and pray for courage. That seemed pretty reasonable.

A few days later, on Valentine's Day, six months and one day before our wedding, the phone rang and we got the results. So sorry, but it's bad news, said the doctor; it was cancer and he was so sure I didn't have cancer but it was cancer, and his voice went on and on as the kitchen tilted. I felt like I was in a very bad movie. And we all know that the minute somebody gets cancer in a movie, her days are numbered.

Having a lumpectomy is an outpatient procedure, kind of a drive-by operation, and not terribly serious, as things go in a hospital. Unless, of course, it's your breast they're operating on, your own personal cancer they're carving out. I made an appointment for the lumpectomy to take place the following week. After the surrounding tissue was biopsied, I'd know what the rest of my treatment would be.

I'd always thought of my body in terms of *if only:* If only my legs were longer, my thighs thinner; if only my hair were thicker, my eyes different, my skin perfect. Oddly, one of the few parts of my body I was fine with was my breasts. They were small, but that was okay; they'd been able to do what they were designed for, and in fact, as I got into my fifties, I was very happy to have little breasts. There wasn't much to droop or sag.

After the lumpectomy, when the tubes and drain were taken out, I looked in the mirror for the first time. My left breast, in spite of its red welts and rainbow-colored bruises, was buoyed up by scar tissue and looked inappropriately perky compared to the healthy one. I knew I was unbelievably lucky that, so far, a lumpectomy was all the treatment I needed, and probably radiation. But would I need chemo and then look like an egg at my wedding, with no hair, no eyebrows? Would I even make it to my wedding, as in *be alive?*

One of the hardest things about having cancer was leaving the old me at the border, the innocent, healthy me, eater of broccoli and tofu, and facing my mortality. The careless, easy relationship with my own health, always taken for granted, suddenly ended. Crossing that border into enemy territory happened for real when I walked through a door marked RADIATION ONCOLOGY. Both words were so foreign to me, so out of context with the rest of my life, that I could have been landing on the moon.

Little black dots were tattooed around my breast as permanent markers of the perimeters of my radiation treatment. I tried to convince the doctor it would be very cool if he'd tattoo some petals around the dots and turn them into daisies. I realized I was obsessed with the idea of being cool because having cancer was so uncool.

A Polaroid was taken for my file. The rainbow colors of my left breast had faded into an alarming shade of yellow, and my new scars, the one under my arm for a lymph node dissection and the two-inch lumpectomy scar by the side of my nipple, still looked serious and raw. I did not look cool. I looked desperate and not terribly sane in this photo; I looked like someone who might appear on the front page of the *Enquirer*.

But radiation, as it turned out, wasn't a big deal. I didn't get tired and my breast didn't burn. For five weeks I would go to the basement of the hospital, to the radiation department, lie down on a table, and get my breast zapped. And I didn't need chemo; I had to count my blessings.

But let me set the record straight here: Getting cancer is not a gift. There are in fact philosophies touting this bizarre idea. And even worse, a belief that somehow you cause your own cancer. I've lost too many friends and relatives to it to find anything giftlike about cancer or to accept the idea that they were somehow terminally careless and caused the disease themselves.

So did cancer make me wake up and smell the coffee, stop and smell the roses? Did I find what didn't kill me made me stronger? Did I change the direction of my life or become a different person?

No; cancer gives you perspective, that's all. Growing old is the gift.

For my sixtieth birthday, R set up a family gathering in Mexico. I walked into a room open to the sea, lit by dozens of tiny candles, my children there to celebrate with us, and someone handed me a cold margarita. I was sixty years old. It was the best birthday of my life.

Full Exposure: What It's Like to Be the
Only Naked Woman in the Room

Elizabeth Rosner

Twenty-five years ago, while an undergraduate at Stanford, I got a job on campus as a lifeguard, deepening a love of swimming and water that has lasted throughout my life. I took the duties seriously and studied the swimmers with professional vigilance, relieved at the end of each day that no emergency rescue had been required. But the greatest challenge of the job was standing poolside in a bathing suit with my body on display.

Work began in the locker room, where I changed into my Speedo and surveyed my reflection, assessing what would be on view for the next few hours. I was plagued by self-criticism. I imagined the swimmers judging my shape, until I made myself remember that I was there to guard their lives, not their fantasies. Later I performed my variation of the same ablutions everyone else did, showering and hair washing, applying lotion and makeup—preparations for reentering the other world of walking upright on solid land.

One day I noticed a young woman with a sketch pad in the locker room. I'M AN ART STUDENT, a handwritten sign read. I'M

HERE FOR THE NATURAL LIGHT AND VARIETY OF FORMS. I HOPE I WON'T BOTHER YOU. I was enthralled by the idea of looking at the room full of bodies in a new way. Undressing and bathing and redressing in a steady stream of movements, we were a palette of skin colors and shapes, a beautiful parade of muses. All the same and each unique: rounder or leaner, taller or shorter, full breasted or flat, with or without bellies, muscle tone. Amazed, I began to picture myself along with the others in my own simple perfection—not as an object measured against impossible standards, but only and purely myself, translated into lines and shadings on a white page. Here was a glimpse of what it was like to be gazed at in the name of art, used as inspiration for beauty, even me.

The artist, Diane, told me about life-drawing classes on campus and, to my own surprise, I asked if any models were needed. I wondered if this could cure the self-consciousness that tormented me. I hoped to learn how to be kinder to myself, replacing a practice of scrutiny and punishment with some renewed belief in the softness of flesh on bone, in the beauty of a curve.

I made the arrangements and went to the classroom at the appointed hour. I offered myself up: the only naked woman in the room. Nervous, terrified, delivered, exhausted. In my haste to dress at the end of class, I left behind my bathrobe. Afterward, I told myself how interesting it had been, how good for me, but I never found the courage to go back for the robe. I walked around campus as usual, but whenever I saw a student from that evening, I felt exposed all over again.

The full classroom had been too overwhelming. Still, something had begun. I found myself looking for a private modeling job. When I replied to an ad in the college paper from an artist named Ken, who was in search of a model, he insisted I call his wife, who worked at Stanford, to reassure me he was safe.

Unlike the experience of modeling for my peers in the classroom, the formality of Ken's studio helped further my sense that he was a professional. At first, disrobing, I pretended to be relaxed, and eventually the pretense became true. Ken made a series of sketches and photographs in preparation for a sculpture of my torso. Often I slept during the long reclining poses, but I remember the ache of holding my arms over my head while he photographed me from the neck down. Eventually, he began the sculpture—a nearly life-size block of clay that slowly and unmistakably took on the appearance of my nude body.

We barely spoke. Even before I really looked at his images of me, I thought about what the drawings and renditions might reveal; if someone else could forgive my imperfections, perhaps I could forgive my own. When I said I would be graduating soon, Ken gave me photographs of my silhouetted torso in black-and-white and color shots of the finished sculpture: front, back, and sides. I tried to see what he might have seen: contours and dimensions, a graceful and anonymous arc in space.

All these years later, the photos remain in my desk drawer, vivid and strange. On occasion, since working with Ken, I have searched again for some elusive reconciliation with myself by modeling for other artists. Each time, I have found a bit of reassurance in the artist's gaze. It's as if I'm being immunized against the diseases spread by magazine covers and movies. But I still struggle to make a more permanent peace with my body, the one I've been given and so often long to shrink or elongate or make closer to perfect. Even now, it's only the water that feels utterly welcoming and without judgment. Immersed, I am a self that is more than the sum of my parts. My edges dissolve. I float.

This essay first appeared in The New York Times Magazine, *May 28, 2006.*

Feel the Pain

Clea Simon

T hat girl down there must be hurting. She hasn't asked for
novocaine. Has specifically rejected it, as a matter of fact.
But the whine of the drill and the dry, smoky smell of the tooth
being ground away must be getting to her. Or so you'd think, but
she doesn't seem to mind.

That girl has already been through so much. Grown-up,
almost, and defiant in her black clothes and her taut, muscular
body. A tomboy, a tough girl. But not always. She can recall, as
if in a home movie, the day her sister killed her hamster. In her
mind, the film plays back, the speed slightly off, the image jumpy
and scarred, pre-videotape, the color aged into yellowing. She is
sitting on the piano bench by her sister. She isn't happy. What
eight-year-old wants to play with a teenage sister? That sister,
anyway, the odd one. The violent one. What shy girl—and the
little redhead prefers to keep to herself—seeks out a game that
scares her, a game she fears will end badly? But she goes along with
her sister's plan, to keep everything quiet, to keep the peace.

There's a photo of her from this time, her bright red curls held back by fake tortoiseshell barrettes. Her chubby body enveloped in a pink and white lace dress. That might not be what she's wearing as she sits on the piano bench, but her chubby hands are the same. Pink, dimpled, they are holding her hamster, Honeybun. Soft and warm. Golden furred, with big dark eyes and an inquisitive nose as pink as that dress, Honeybun is the love of her life. Her own sweet darling. And it is fun to see him run, his precise little feet bare beneath his fuzzy bulk.

But it is not fun to see him scared, as his weight depresses a piano key for a loud *whoom* of sound. It is not fun to see him uneasy, each seemingly solid step giving way beneath him, causing more of those loud, unnerving noises.

So why does she do it? Holding up her hands in a wall along the outside of the keyboard. Creating a corridor of keys between the piano and her hands, so her little pet has no choice, will stay on the piano, where each step is a thundering *boom*. Why does she do it, when she's tensing up, too, waiting for the louder noise? Waiting for her own world to fall through?

When the final crash comes, she is almost ready. She does not have to glance up to know the look in her sister's eyes. She does not want to see her glee, her impulse. The madness. She does not have to, but she does not want to look at her pet, either. Her soft, sweet playmate crushed by the sudden closing of the keyboard cover. Honeybun is gone. He will live for hours yet, lying in a shoebox lined with cotton, their mother's pale attempt at comfort. But Honeybun is gone, just like she is gone. Like she has learned to disappear from that pink, chubby girl, from the impulse to scream, to rage, to yell, "No! No! No!" It's just easier somehow, and she continues like that.

After a while, her sister is gone from the house, and she remembers only the long drives. Her parents are silent, and that helps the time pass. Looking out the window, as the highway whips by, she imagines a life out in those woods. She could be a wildcat, a panther, racing along. Only this wouldn't be a highway, it would be a river, and she'd be stretching her long, leonine limbs for the fun of it. She'd be tall and lean, tough and tight. There'd be no end in sight. No family meetings. No hospital. She wouldn't be a little girl, a soft, round little girl. She'd be an animal. Ferocious and unafraid.

Pot helps, once she gets to her teens. Like Pink Floyd sings it, she's "comfortably numb." Only years afterward, when the memories are fuzzy and she realizes how few close friends she has made, will she wonder how she passed the time. How the days went by. She isn't a panther then, but other roles come and go. In class she's an honor student. She knows she studies more than most and that many of her classmates find her odd. That's okay. It's because she's smart.

After a while, she became a musician. The loud rock she played seemed comforting somehow. The louder, the better. And if she didn't fit in, well, she didn't expect to. She was a young woman in what was still the very macho rock world. She was a smart kid hanging out with the stoners. She'd have fit in in Narnia, maybe, but not suburbia.

Sure, things got through to her. Once she got to college, she realized there were other oddballs around. Smart kids who smoked pot. Gentle people who played even louder music. And their music—wow, that touched something. "We're desperate. Get used to it," sang X and Mike from Los Angeles, who introduced the band to her and became her friend. "The world's a mess, it's in my kiss." She opened up, enough anyway to fall tragically, desperately in love with one of Mike's friends. There was something there, something permanent. She could feel it. She could feel!

When it didn't work, she thought of her body. Was it there, still, the round pink flesh under the pink dress? She starved herself. Watched her thighs shrink, her cheekbones emerge. Learned the caloric value of half a tangerine and how many miles it took to run off a Ring Ding. She didn't even like Ring Dings, or the easier equivalent: a fake chocolate roll with a white cream filling that tasted of grease and cost $1.29 at Louie's Superette. She could be there and back in eight minutes. It was open until eleven. All numbers, the price of success. Numbers on the scale became points, and she was keeping score. Budgeting. She would win. Food became a commodity to be taken in or rejected.

She went after him. Sometimes she got him, sometimes not. More often not, as time went by, and she blamed her body. It had failed, lost its allure, and she sought to desex herself. Punk was hard, all edges. She hated softness in herself, any softness she saw or felt, and she drank for a while. Even that became pointless. No matter how much you drank, you woke up. And it had so many calories. Years later, she'd realize that he, too, came from a silent home. Mom was paranoid, tried to kill herself. Had maybe tried to kill her son, too, which could have explained the distance. No matter; at the time it hurt too much. She let go. Went back into herself. The music alone would be enough.

She graduated, started working. Found a way to hear the music, to write about the music. That was the only part of life that had any heat to it. It was lean, hard. She worked at eliminating excess. The music, the writing. Everything else was only to maintain. Only she wasn't maintaining. She was slipping. The pointless connections became briefer; the nightmares, worse. The clock was slowing down.

She couldn't remember what made her call. It could have been the night the guy left and she realized she didn't even like him. That her body had taken no pleasure, that lump of white softness that she had to claim as hers. It might have been the crying. She hated the way her sobs made her belly jiggle, and she was crying a lot. Sometimes she woke up with her face wet.

At any rate, she'd tried therapy before. But this time it worked. At least, it tapped into something. For months, she cried every week. When they upped her sessions to twice a week, she cried harder. Could it have been her family? Could she have been scared? Nonsense, she had had a lock on her door, a little hook-and-eye thing that she could put on whenever she wanted to be alone. If she did the lock and sat very quietly, in the closet, holding still, being small, her sister wouldn't even know she was there.

She cried some more. She was beginning to realize she was different. Not like her sister, no, that nightmare had come and gone. Although she still envied her sister's thinness, her sleek blond slimness. She was big, white, and pink. An easy target. Just what she didn't want. But she was tougher than the others around her, and with her punk ethos it made her proud. Blood? Cleans up easy, no matter how crazy the party. Just use cold water so it won't stain the walls. Sleep was a choice. Without sleep, she lost weight. The disgusting bulges receded. She didn't need drugs; it was all will. She could do more, work harder, and still drive to New York to catch that last set. Breakfast in Connecticut was a luxury earned. A dry bagel, coffee, and the sun rising as she made it back home.

And at the dentist? Piece of cake. She just . . . stepped back from the scene. But why? she remembers the dentist asking her. Why would she choose to feel the drill? This was a serious cavity. She'd be lucky if he could save the tooth.

She knew about serious cavities. She could have laughed. There was no pain. He did touch a nerve, though, with his question. Why would she not take the comfort? Several years into therapy, she was learning to turn the questions inward. It made for an interesting intellectual exercise. Why had she gone that route?

It was the equilibrium, she decided. Pain, she knew. She could anticipate what would happen, what she would—or would not—feel. Give her a shot, alter the situation—that was uncertain. That was giving someone else control. That was scary.

How could she be afraid? Tough. Leathery in her soul. Yes, the body was soft. Too soft, repulsive. But she didn't give an inch. She could fight back.

Maybe that's why the class intrigued her. She'd not wanted to go. It was a workmate, a woman she didn't like much. Too . . . emotional. Whiny. Soft. But the round little blond had signed up and done the time and now she was graduating. And the office was going. If nothing else, she had learned to fit in. It was easier. She went. She was wowed. There was that butterball, that chubby little . . . girl . . . kicking a man, an attacker, a huge, cushioned creature, off the mat. Kicking, hitting. Hard hard hard!

It took another year. Maybe two; the time was flying. She was in another relationship. She didn't know why it wasn't working. He was fat. Soft, repulsive. He wanted all her time. That was the conflict. She wanted to go out, to hear music. There were people she called friends. Music people who understood the draw. He didn't. He wanted to control her. He was disgusting, all she deserved. But she wanted to kick. Hard.

She signed up for the class. It was something she could do, a reason she could give for not being in his apartment. She went half thinking she would leave or not return. The first day was a lot of talk. What was our worst fear? What were our nightmares? Others talked about rape. About abusive spouses who broke their teeth. She didn't know what to say. Talked about her boyfriend. But he was soft, clinging. They did some exercises, went over the basics. Women, the instructors explained, tended to have more lower-body strength. We kick better than we punch. This is where our weight is. Our strength.

She had always hated her bottom. Too big, too soft. A source of strength? Not likely. But she tried it. She kicked.

She yelled when they told her to, hearing her voice deepen and grow. The high, tight sound became bigger. "Kick!" She heard her classmates cheer her on. "Face!" Her fingers, bunched, went for the face mask, where the eyes would be. "Kick! Go, go, *go!*" She punched and kicked and felt the wild thrill of success. He fell. He stumbled. He flew off the mat. After two sessions, she was an animal. A creature of power.

The boyfriend didn't have a chance. She called him, breathless, unwilling to wait. It was over. She needed out. Space. To take a deep breath into her belly and let it out. He was history.

And he was there, at her apartment. He had a key. She heard the sound and shrank back, ready to be quiet. To be nothing. To be not there. But something had changed. She was big. Too big—but that was okay. He came in, angry, looming. Fat but also tall. And she looked up at him, and a small voice told her quietly, *I could hurt him if I had to.*

She pulled herself up to her full height. Almost as tall as he was. Broad, strong. "I need you to leave." He backed down, unsure. She repeated herself. "I need you to leave." She felt the strength in her back. In her hips, her wide, anchoring hips, and her legs. "And I need my keys back."

"I need my keys back." I said it, and he left. And I and my hips and my heavy, muscled legs had done it. When I graduated from the class a week later, it felt almost anticlimactic. Sure, I got into the rush of the fight. I drove my "attacker" off the mat, and I roared with the class as we cheered each other on. "Kick! Yell! Face! Kick! *Kick!*" I cried, we all did. I cry today, writing about it, fifteen years later. I feel my belly tighten up as I sob, and I know that only my jeans—my black jeans, under my black long-sleeve T-shirt—hold in my tum. My "tum." My husband's word. Soft, but also sweet.

Like Honeybun. They say that children identify with their pets. That we see ourselves in these small, dependent animals, so much more vulnerable, like children, than any around us. So much softer. When my sister killed Honeybun, she was threatening me. Small wonder, then, that I opted out. That I rejected the soft sweetness of my little girl's body and all the softness that was to come. Small wonder that I sought control at any price.

Is the trauma gone? Have I learned to live in my body yet, with all its roundness and curves? Well, I've made peace at least, as much as any woman in today's culture can. I watch what I eat, halfheartedly, but I enjoy cheese and sweets and a good bottle of wine. I try to treasure myself and keep in mind that I've faced worse enemies. My sister cannot harm me now. She can barely take care of herself and cycles in and out of halfway houses. I pity her now, in a distant way, although the memory—the idea—of her still scares me too much to want her close. She, and the others I have let near me, have inflicted enough harm through the years, and so I try not to do it myself. I try not to beat myself up over the pounds that have crept onto my waist, my thighs, and those strong, wide hips. Sometimes I'm even proud of them. Them? Of *myself*, my body. I've faced scarier enemies than the mirror. These days, if I see myself in that girl—that poor, scared girl—I try to give her some comfort, some acceptance, and some hope. I know she felt the pain.

Making Joy and Love in Seasoned Bodies
Joan Price

"Oh-oh-oh!" are my first words of the day. No, I'm not in the throes of sexual passion; I'm testing which body parts work as I get out of bed. A knife twists through my shoulder as I reach to turn on the lamp. My knee barely bends—a giant pair of pliers has twisted it askew during the night. My right foot is a concrete block with no ankle motion. It can't bear my weight yet, so I hop and hobble toward the bathroom. This is my sixty-three-year-old morning body.

"Oh-oh-oh!" I hear Robert call out as he tests his back, fractured ten months ago; his feet and ankles, worn down by decades of dancing; his shoulder, chronically sore from a lifetime as an abstract artist.

We dissolve into laughter as our "oh-oh-ohs" blend in harmony. Our vocalizations have become part of our morning ritual to greet the day and each other, and we make it a game, chiming together over the woes of each day's first steps in aging bodies. Laughter, we know, is healing.

Love and exercise are also healing, and Robert and I know that by walking the park this afternoon, or teaching a line-dance class this evening, or making love later this morning, our bodies will become more energetic and youthful as the day goes on. Our bodies are strengthened each day by our determination, physical activity, emotional resilience, and joie de vivre.

*   *   *

November 1979

My vision froze on the oncoming car fishtailing across both lanes, headlights aiming for me. No time to escape, no place to go. Before I could even scream, the metal beast leaped into my path and crunched my car into me. My blood-filled eyes watched the windshield crinkle into rose-colored crystals.

I never totally lost consciousness. My perceptions blurred and drifted, slow motion. *A dream,* I thought, unable to make sense of my surroundings. I tried to shift positions, but the car door was caved in around me. I couldn't move forward because the steering wheel had smashed against my face. I couldn't turn my head: a neck fracture. My jaw, broken in six places, would not move. My right foot seemed fastened to the floor: My own bone had impaled it, and my heel had been shattered. Yes, I was seat belted, or I would not have lived to write this.

"We don't know how you survived the first hour," my doctor told me later. "We see one case like yours a year; the rest don't make it to the hospital."

I'm still convinced that two years of daily aerobics classes and cycling had conditioned my heart well enough to go on automatic pilot while I waited for help. Most important, I had decided to live.

A week after the accident, the swelling had gone down enough to operate. "We know we can put your face back together," my doctor assured me, "but your foot will be harder. You'll be able to walk, but maybe not normally or pain free. You won't have full motion."

"I don't care about walking normally," I said. "I want to dance."

Four doctors pieced me back together for seven hours, repairing my neck fracture and broken wrist, rebuilding my shattered foot, and reconstructing my smashed face from photographs, wiring together the myriad tiny, broken bones.

January 2007

It's a new experience, living in a body that feels old. Nicknamed "Miss Perky" by my fitness clients years ago, I've always been upbeat and energetic, no matter what life deals me, and I still manage that most of the time. But my body surprises me every day: What parts will and won't work today? Which parts will and won't hurt today? Old pains retreat and recur, new aches surface, and I am daily proof that the adage is true: The only way not to lose it is to use it.

That goes for sex, too. I fretted during my often-sexless single years, in my forties and fifties, that I would never again have the opportunity to express the hot sexuality that had been so much a part of my younger life. I filled my bedside drawer with sex toys, but they just took the edge off the immediate physical urge—they were lousy at cuddling or making me laugh or providing the bonding I felt by giving pleasure to my lover.

Then, at age fifty-seven, it happened. I was teaching my contemporary line-dance class one winter evening when a strikingly handsome and fit sixty-three-year-old man with dazzling blue eyes and white hair entered my class. The lust center of my brain did cartwheels the first time he moved his slim, mobile hips in rhythm with the dance. I learned later that he had been a dancer since childhood.

I didn't know at the time that Robert would dance his way into my heart. I just knew that when he moved on the dance floor, I wanted to touch him, feel the softness of the tuft of chest hair peeking from the V of his shirt. I wanted to hold his hips as they swayed sensuously. *How would he smell close up?* I wondered. *How would his kiss taste? How would his graceful hands move on me?* I was in raging lust.

It took nine months before we became lovers. At first, the more assertively I pursued him, the faster he backed away, always polite but never seeming to return my interest.

Finally, I propositioned him.

He turned me down.

Hours later, by email, he changed his mind.

In the next few days, we shared our first date, our first kiss, our first exploratory touches, and our first languid afternoon as lovers. Our lovemaking was surprisingly tender and intense. We bonded. We fell in love.

How joyful and thrilling it was to cascade into love and exhilarating sex at our age! We were as giddy and frisky as a couple of teenagers but with the added richness of decades of experience and self-knowledge. In fact, it was, and continues to be, the best sex I have ever experienced.

We take lots and lots of time. Two hours is a "date," one hour is a "quickie." (Or, as we call it in our private language, a "cookie.") As younger women, didn't we always wish for more foreplay? Now we can get it, because our partners enjoy it as much as we do. There's no rush to the finish at our age. It's the journey we both enjoy, the gradually rising sensuality, and the ability to make it last is one of the great joys of older-age sexuality.

Does that mean that older-age sex is, for me, just as juicy as younger sex? No, certainly not physically. The reason we take so long is that we *have to*, or it doesn't work. My sensual responses are much slower and require a much more concerted effort by my partner to get me aroused. Arousal is elusive: If we don't take enough time, or touch softly or slowly enough, or kiss long enough, it just doesn't happen. At first I was embarrassed by how long it took me to become aroused and then reach orgasm, and, silly me, I apologized to Robert, thinking he might be bored.

"I don't care if it takes two weeks," he told me, "as long as I can take a break once in a while to change positions and get something to eat."

November 1979

When they first let me try crutches, I was so weak that I could only wobble for a few seconds and then slide back into my wheelchair. But I practiced, making a game of setting goals each hour at first and then each day as I got stronger.

For the first week, I could leave my bed accompanied only, so I greeted my visitors with "Help me walk?" My friends attached my neck brace, a complex metal-and-plastic contraption that was strapped around my chest and back to hold my head and neck immobile. Then they helped me slide out of bed, fastened my right arm onto a special platform crutch, handed me my other crutch, and held on to me as I tried to maneuver. I was a strange sight, clunking down the hospital halls, and even stranger when people got close enough to see the wires coming out of my eyebrows—wires that held my mending facial bones in place under my skin.

As soon as I was strong enough to be trusted on my own, I planned my day around my walking. I'd get to the nurses' station and back and then would have to nap before trying it again. Talk about taking it one step at a time! I was delirious with happiness to be alive and, in my limited way, active again. I also found that determination and physical activity were better painkillers than Demerol.

I became agile on crutches and during the course of a year I progressed from crutches to a cane. Then I abandoned the cane and worked at strengthening my foot enough to lessen my clumsy limp. Through all this, I danced. Even while I was still on crutches, I did one-legged aerobics at the health club, holding on to the ballet barre as I hopped my way through the instructor's routine.

Throughout this long healing experience of learning to walk again, I kept seeing people who *could* walk but chose *not* to, who *could* run and dance but chose to be sedentary. I vowed then that *when*, not if, I recovered, my mission would be to share the joy of movement. Through the years, I became an aerobics instructor and then a line-dance instructor. I became a personal trainer, specializing in helping beginners make exercise a habit. I also became a professional speaker, sharing my story with audiences.

January 2007

When I was young and at the height of my sexuality, a single touch would catapult all my sexual response centers into a tsunami of sensuality. I would feel the tingles and shivers escalate until I became one huge, crashing wave. It's different now. At first I feel like I'm watching the waves from afar, through a smudged window. I know what they're like close up, but it takes a long journey to become part of them. In addition, even when I'm aroused, my intimate parts seldom lubricate on their own. I'm emotionally ready to go, but the physiological response lags.

So with all that going on—or *not* going on—how can I profess to be having the best sex of my life? Simple: These challenges bring us closer. Since we can't depend on the physiological responses that used to be almost automatic, we have to tune in to each other strongly, communicate clearly, and laugh a lot. We kiss and kiss, reveling in the intimacy of our mouths and hearts coming together. And what about all those "oh-oh-oh!" physical challenges? We've learned creativity in finding positions and props that let us forget our aging body parts.

November 1995

Although living in an aging body is new for me, living in an injured one, unfortunately, is not. I wish I could say this story ended with my recovery from that first crash, but sixteen years later, the unthinkable occurred.

It happened again.

I was five minutes from home, returning from teaching line-dance at a convention in San Francisco. I saw a car come toward me, miss the bend in the road, and cut in front of me. If the driver had continued, he would have gone into a ditch. But no, he overcorrected, and I couldn't get out of the way in time. I reacted reflexively and put my foot on the brake. Then came the sickening sound of metal smashing metal.

Silence. I looked down past my bloody knee at the foot I had so carefully rehabilitated for sixteen years, the one that had pushed the brake at the moment of impact. It hung off my leg at an impossible right angle, dangling as if hanging on by skin alone.

"It's a very, very bad break," the doctor told me in the hospital. My shinbones were practically severed.

"What's the worst-case scenario?" I asked.

"Amputation," he answered.

But my surgeon was a miracle worker who was able to repair my shins and reconstruct my ankle . . . again. For months, I screamed from the pain of healing: My leg felt like it was wrapped in thorny brambles pressed into my skin with a hot iron. Anything touching the skin of my leg was intolerable, as if all the nerve endings were on the outside. Even a soft sheet resting lightly on my leg felt razor sharp. My painkillers dulled the pain only enough for nightmare-ridden, fitful sleep.

Although I had fewer injuries this time, the rehabilitation was harder, maybe because I was older, maybe because I had been through it before and knew how long and painful the process would be. As soon as I was well enough to request it, my friends drove me to the gym, where I did everything I could manage with two arms and one leg; and to the park, where I hobbled joyfully on crutches until I was exhausted, welcoming the sun on my face and the feeling of my body's moving again. Eventually, I even taught line-dance on crutches. (A student told me, "You should charge extra for that.")

January 2007

Today I am one of the happiest and luckiest people I know. My leg, foot, and ankle still give me pain, and I limp when I do too much or too little, but most people who take my line-dance class or accompany me on a walk would never guess what I've endured. I've added to my residual accident pain the new physical challenges of aging: arthritis; a knee and hip that sometimes flare; and the beginnings of osteoporosis. But I apply what I learned from accident number one to everything I do: Keep moving; keep making progress; and celebrate being alive in a body that lets me dance and love.

I agree with Helen Keller that we can't always determine what happens to us, but we sure can determine what we do about it. Since accident number two, I have fallen in love and married, written six books and scores of articles, motivated hundreds of people to exercise and dance, and reveled in the joy of movement. I see each day, each hour, as a gift I might never have had. I'm never bored, never idle. I'm aware every hour of my life that I almost lost it. I cannot put one foot in front of the other without marveling at the wonder of it. I never take for granted the strength of my feet to bear my weight or the ability of my legs to move me.

Each time I dance or make love or even walk across a room, I feel delight at having the power to move my body, to train and strengthen it, to enjoy movement for its own sake. Sharing this story also brings me joy, as birthdays pass that I might not have celebrated, with loved ones I might never have known.

Holes

Abby Frucht

Except that it costs me my whole deductible, I enjoy my hysterectomy. I find hospitals stimulating. I like the funk of anesthesia, and I'm amused by the bright-blue nun, like on the wine bottle label, who stops by at pre-op to pray. I'm proud of the tumor they get out of me, and I love that my friends bring me lavender oil and my son serves me dinner when I go home to heal.

Though I'm a reader and a writer, I prefer CNN, the way my dull pelvic pain and the world's sharper sufferings coalesce in a haze of morphine and pills. We'll cancel each other out, I imagine. If I'm hurting inside, then what's happening outside will distract me. And when bad things happen outside, then what's happening inside will protect me. At four o'clock every day, I'll walk the dog around the block, gauging my agility along the uneven sidewalks. I'll cook my healthful meals and write my peculiar stories and collect my son from school and call my other son at college, keeping things neat and appealing, functional. If, as the doctor orders, I lift no sack of groceries and vacuum no floor, I'll be back at the YMCA in no time, doing my crazed aerobics, my skinny-legged jumping jacks.

But then . . . then . . . the strangest thing.

I remember giving birth, my water breaking on a hospital-waiting-room chair.

Rather, my body remembers.

Really, no, the couch remembers. The battered love seat, with its mattress-ticking cover, remembers.

Water breaks on it.

My body awash, as if floating there, coolly regarding the too-white ceiling. I pay no heed to the burgeoning war on television, no heed to the love seat, no heed to the fog rising out of the cushions.

It won't happen again.

"You won't pee your pants again," Wolf Blitzer instructs.

"No," agrees Christiane Amanpour, "she won't."

I do.

*   *   *

Two days later, I haven't yet told my boyfriend I'm peeing my pants, and, even when my son is at his dad's house, I don't ask Chuck over. Instead, I try to do what the doctor advises when he finally returns my telephone call. It's the same advice the nurses gave me when, impatient to hear from the doctor, I dialed the incontinence clinic. "Try to regulate the times you sit on the toilet," they all say to me. "Go every two hours. No more, no less. And when you can make it to two hours without any spotting, stretch it to two and a half. Be sure to do your Kegels. And how many glasses of water did you say you've been drinking, again?"

"Six a day," I say, relieved that they have not told me to give in and buy diapers or pads. "You're barely in your forties. You don't want to train your body to rely on Pampers," they scold. "You want to learn to hold it in."

But though I squeeze and squeeze and squeeze, still the urine streams out. Alone, I lay a towel across the mattress, and in the middle of the night I spread a dry towel next to the soaked-through one. Come morning, I scoop a third towel between my legs to catch the deluge of pee on my rush to the toilet.

There is no sense in rushing, no sense in toilets at all. There is only this upended pitcher that I struggle to imagine is in my control—a woman driving to the mall on a folded towel, intent on buying a new winter coat that will share space with the doctor on the credit card bills. See her marching through the mall, wearing her cowboy boots with the quilted lining, squeezing and squeezing as diligently as she can. She makes her way to Wilsons Leather, drops her purse at the mirror. This season, the coats are like animal skins. She likes the inside-out sheep, the outside-in lamb. But her corduroy pants with their knuckly crotch provide inadequate camouflage. There's a drenching of urine, the very heat of it weighing the pants far down. Maybe her frantic exchanging of hangers, the way she tugs at the toggles, flings off the skins, rounds up another five—maybe *this* is camouflage.

The girls at the counter wrinkle their noses, stifle their horror. I imagine them making their casual way to a bathroom, relieving themselves. I imagine them wiping, drying themselves. Every woman I see, I think of this.

* * *

Women in developing countries suffer far more vesicovaginal fistulas than in developed ones, usually as a result of childbearing rather than hysterectomy, and, despite the aid available to them, they are rarely as lucky as I would be. Many are flung away by family and society, outcasts forever, suffering constant infection and dripping urine or feces wherever they roam.

In the United States, repairs are easy to come by, although, because of the tenderness of the damaged flesh, you need to wait some time to be successfully stitched back up again. In my case, five months would pass between the day my shamefaced doctor, wearing one of his Disney bandannas—Dumbo for surgery, Daffy for making hospital rounds—finally owned up to having scraped a hole between my bladder and my vagina, and the day Chuck drove me three hundred miles to the Mayo Clinic for repair.

I don't actually need to tell Chuck I'm peeing my pants; instead, I tuck a wedge of toilet paper inside two pairs of panties under my jeans and sit beside him on his new leather couch in his carpeted TV room. I don't actually believe that the TP will work; on the other hand, I don't really believe that I'll pee again, either. Every trickle that comes I think is the last, certain that the Kegel exercises I learned on the Internet will put a stopper in me. Squeeze, hold, count to ten. Squeeze, hold, count to ten. But, as happened when I tried Kegels years ago after birthing, they only make me want sex.

Chuck is the sanest person I know and laid-back enough that my weeklong avoidance of spending the night raises no alarm. I don't jump up when I flood his couch, and when the leathery runnels make their way to Chuck's half, where they form bleak, steamy ponds that sluice onto the carpet, he doesn't jump up, either. He simply meets my eyes. Clearly, he suspected. Maybe he's smelled it on me, has seen my agitation, my furtive changing of clothes, the way I cock my head and listen when he stands at the toilet, amazed at the voluminous ease of it, the precise start-and-stop of it.

"I'd say it's time to buy diapers," Chuck suggests gently, giving a nod to my soaked-through jeans.

"But what if there's nothing they can do about it?" I ask, flapping my hands at my crotch and bursting into tears for the very first time. "What if I'm like this forever?"

But I soon calm down. There's a story I remember, about some people who hired a cook and asked her to serve honeydew melon, a fruit she'd neither seen nor eaten before. When fifteen minutes went by, she emerged from the kitchen bearing a deep bowl of pulp and seeds, and a silver ladle. Chuck understands that, because I'm a writer, I might indulge in the thought of that bowl of juices, sweet but wasted, the seeds floating in goo, and that the image might trick me into feeling a little better. I'm not a woman pissing through her vagina when I remember that bowl. Instead I'm a sodden, spongy fruit, a dropped peach with torn skin. I can almost find her funny and beautiful then, the woman buying diapers at Kmart the next day, shyly proclaiming to the checkout line that the diapers are for Grandma.

"If there's nothing they can do about it, we'll live with it, hon," Chuck answers. Then he draws me a bath, brings me thick towels, puts my jeans in his laundry, and fetches me a T-shirt that reaches to my knees.

*   *   *

Back in June we had arranged for a trip to Jamaica, but by the time winter comes, our romantic getaway is far different than we'd expected. At departure, it's I they single out for a random search of my carry-on, which holds a week's worth of ladies' petite diapers that pile up on the table in view of the other passengers. Aside from at mealtimes, I've little intention of wearing them, for I regard this trip as a chance to leak, unnoticed, into the salty atmosphere. I long to feel the air around me again. Swimming, aware of the ocean seeping into my body through the extra incision it has been granted, I'm like a gladdened jellyfish slopping around. The bladder infections that accompany the fistula are quickly soothed, and, though I leave a trail behind me wherever I go, it might as well be seawater soaking my droopy sarong.

As for our sex life, suffice it to say that penetration is forbidden for an entire half year; that I don't blame Chuck for not exactly hungering for going down on me; and that I feel just sore enough that I don't much want him to. I want only to cuddle skin to skin in that long lazy hour between beach and supper, padding barefoot now and then to the chairs outside our room. Every time I sit on one of those chairs, pee gushes through the slats with the flat noise of sheet rain striking the tiles, but Chuck goes on peaceably nursing his cigarette, holding my hand, asking if I mind his turning up the TV volume inside so we can hear the ski races and admire the ocean at the same time. Between slaloms we turn to CNN, where the war is growing dirtier, nastier. Against the spectacle of such athleticism, and then such cruel barbarity, I understand I am at least appropriately bestial, dripping and stinking, wounded, open, filled with scary, raw emotion. I weep at the carnage, and I am frightened of my Mayo Clinic repair, scheduled for March. No matter how I long to be normal again, to be all at once healed will be like a song ending too soon on a radio. You want it to last you the whole way home. You don't want it to end before you know what it takes to feel like part of the human race again.

*   *   *

Because one diaper never lasts a whole night, my doctor now and then suggests that I try to get by with a catheter instead. It's a "walking" catheter, which means you carry the bag on the end of the tube like a shoulder-strap pocketbook, only lower than your bladder, lest the urine slide back where it came from. The first tube is too wide—it hurts so much that I need to be rushed to the hospital. And the smaller tube leaks.

What I like about those catheters is that you clean them with vinegar. You use the plain white vinegar from the gallon jug with the pictures of cabbage and onions on it. First thing in the morning, you empty the urine out of the catheter into the toilet, and then you fit a dented aluminum funnel to the end of the tube, and then you fill the synthetic bladder and the coiling tube with vinegar before letting them steep awhile and clothespinning them up in the shower to dry. Pretty soon, the house reeks of vinegar. In a way you hate the smell, but in a way you get a thrill from that humble funnel, and from how basic and inexpensive the vinegar is, and from how many centuries it's been around, and you wonder what her name was and how she did up her hair and how many people she was feeding for supper and how she lived and died—that first farmwife who dressed that first cucumber with fermented wine—and how on earth they got from there to disinfecting catheters.

After the Mayo Clinic repair, I need to be catheterized again for three days, but the tube, instead of running through the urethra, snakes through my lower abdomen like a confused umbilicus, causing no pain at all and leaking not even a drop. When it's time to remove it, I unclamp the balloon, wait until it deflates, and give a slow, steady pull until the tube slides free and there is left amid my pubic hair a small clenched mouth that will soon disappear. I sterilize the catheter twice with vinegar and coil it up in a shoebox full of doctor toys to be saved for the grandchildren, whoever they are. There are a roll of bandaging, a handful of swabs, the aluminum funnel, those funny hospital socks, and a graduated cylinder.

Eventually, I'll move with my boys into a house with Chuck and his old dad and sell my house to a lady who likes everything about it except for the color I had that too-white ceiling painted back in November. Ripe persimmons are a deep, rich, nectary, puckery orange, and when my son and I lie tangled beneath that color on the striped, ruined love seat once I am healed (he wouldn't snuggle up with me when I was in diapers), most often we turn on the news, but sometimes we don't, and sometimes we talk about how we are feeling, but often we don't. It's okay to not know everything that's happening to everyone all the time, I figure, as long as we know that whatever it is, we are porous in the face of it. For we are made of tiny openings, of freshly rended passageways. Sometimes they're painful, and often they're messy, and now and then they make you fall completely apart, and that's what they're for.

Visit www.worldwidefistulafund.org if you're able to help.

Joyride

Katia Noyes

When I was in my twenties, I believed physical pain needed to be met with absurd abandon or simply ignored. I reached the same conclusion (surprise!) in my ripe forties, albeit in a more gentle and lighthearted way. I found ways to cope with pain that flew in the face of what I'd been told by therapists and by books that informed me that *pain was a teacher* and I needed to *listen*. Desperation, as it turned out, was my teacher, and she took me into some unexpected places.

When I think of my almost twenty years of back pain, I admit to an urge to slam my head against the wall, one side and then the other. I also admit to a periodic need to escape and give in to existential dread. A flood of anxiety will still make me leave stores, drive home, and greet the top of Miguel Street with delirious relief, knowing that soon I'll be in the comfort of my bed, able to pet my cat, turn on NPR, and numb out with the latest body counts from Iraq.

And where would any of us be without drugstore candy? Plenty of other healthy-living women must enjoy the lure and swoon of heavy drugs. But, thank god, after three days of being high, I'm one of the lucky fools who starts craving real life. I tire of underwater snorkeling expeditions and miss the clean vertical alignment of my body. I need to feel my feet on the ground, want to recognize my friends' voices on the phone. The joy of inebriation is another matter. No matter how bad the stabs of pain, if I have a stiff cocktail and go out with someone whom I adore (that part is important), then I can forget.

Since common therapeutic wisdom has never worked for me, I've compiled my own bag of techniques to cope with pain. After all, I suppose it's one of life's biggest conundrums: How the hell *does* one deal with horrible, searing pain in the heart or body? What do we do when we can't move, when we are stuck, when we want to die?

My story is this: I once was a happy experimental dancer. One of my favorite duets involved throwing myself like a wild animal onto a beautiful man, latching on to him, and then being violently thrown off. Performing for a thousand people or performing for ten, the applause, the sweaty jumps, the nervous extensions, the buildup of flirty rehearsals, the flowers afterward—what a broke and wonderful career I pursued for fifteen years; what a devoted artiste! I was addicted to the adrenaline rush. I don't think I'll ever again experience anything like it. Imagine wild-thing sex, add live music, amp your nerve endings a thousandfold, and then top it all off with an all-night party—and you'll understand my best performance nights.

My story changed slowly. My first back pain started not from dance, ironically, but from being a roofer, bending over to hammer shingles. Roofing was one of the more triumphant jobs I did to support my dance habit, yet it already had repercussions when I was twenty. I continued to have problems with my back, but the worst came when I was in a car accident right before turning thirty. The impact of the crash shattered something deep. I thought the subsequent pain was a lie, and that nothing could ever keep me from dancing, but as it turned out, the pain didn't go away; no amount of willpower would make my situation change.

And here, life gets interesting. What is taken from us, what we lose, the powerful moment of reckoning. *Such an opportunity,* the sages say. I had suffered from unfulfilled ego dreams before, but my new frustrations were off the charts. Rather than fretting about the line of my arch, the range of my extensions, how to find a new dance company, or my confounding lack of world fame, I now worried about how to get sleep, descend from a bed, obtain accessible work, and sometimes even how to breathe. The doctors told me little about why it hurt so much. I wanted to fade away and die in a whimper.

My sweetheart at the time suffered from her own chronic illness. Together we created a womb of safety on Bernal Hill, in a time before people started remodeling with corporate stock–fed fevers. When we looked out the front window, drug dealers pointed up and yelled, "What you looking at?" In response, we retreated to the back bedroom, where I remember the hours of lying on ice, the long, quiet reprieves from life while I stared through a high window at the top of a nearby Catholic church. The steeples, the mission-style red clay tiles, the ethereal cream-colored walls. My world had slowed down, come to a stop. I was no longer a dancer—I was nothing. In response, I desired only safety, a few moments when I didn't hurt.

During this time, I took to a California-girl notion that if I could allow myself to be loved—*let the love in,* as a self-help book might entreat—my back pain would fly away on a million angel wings. On waking each morning, I made it a ritual to caress my girlfriend's butt, nuzzle her neck with its fluff of baby-bird hair, draw in a grateful current of love. It did make me warm and happy, but it did nothing for the stabbing pain.

However, I'm glad to report that through the course of two decades, the pain has changed, and that, more important, I have learned to deal. At a recent party for a literary festival, I danced in naughty splendor for two hours and didn't think a whit about my back. On the other hand, last Christmas Eve the pain returned with a vengeance in response to a glorious ride over bumpy country roads on the back of a Harley-Davidson. (It was worth it.) I never know when it will come; pain visits without an invitation.

For years I've wanted to help others locked in a chronic cycle of pain. I'm not sure it will work, but here's what I've learned, the three basic shifts of attitude to replace the often-useless *embrace the pain, embrace the pain* mantra.

Feel the pain and do it anyway. Back pain made me pull away from life. After my accident in the mid-'80s, I started behaving like a scared hermit. It happened without my realizing it—an accumulation of months, then years, of staring at the church from the back bedroom. I had a job, but I lived to return home each night and seek relief from the pain.

I didn't realize how small my life had become until the day a friend took me to an afternoon party on Potrero Hill. We arrived and wandered among scores of hardcore punk dykes gathered outside a large house. Everybody's clothing had been torn, shredded, or burned into submission. I searched for something to drink among a forest of empty whiskey bottles as deep-dish rap music blared from a boom box. A group of tattooed women grinned at me from an outside couch, where they were sprawled on top of one another. Over on the street, a man in a parked-in car leaned on his horn, gunned his motor, and gave the finger to a drunken but friendly woman who was taking her time moving her truck. Several of her friends, dressed in skirts and holey tights, jumped off the curb and onto the hood of the man's car, howling with defiant glee. Howling, whiskey-drinking, rap-listening, skirt-wearing lesbians? Yes! A vast improvement over sincere plaid shirts and folksy potlucks. As a lifelong lover of mayhem, I was thrilled to see what had been happening with the next generation. The last time I'd been around this many dykes, they had been grumpy and sunburned, sitting quietly near a polluted river while listening to an expensive sex therapist.

The moral of my story? If you let pain keep you inside a low-rent apartment for a couple of years, you may miss an entire turn of the zeitgeist wheel. The world will leave you behind. To get back into life, I decided to feel the pain and go out anyway. I stopped making pain a primary factor in my choice of activities.

From what I understand now, the physiology of chronic pain (as opposed to new, acute pain) means that the neurons will cling to established pathways. Sure, they flare up from real damage, but they respond just as much to familiar pain circuits. Although physical damage remains, chronic pain can arrive without much cause. It's a tricky beast. Like emotional depression, old pain returns again and again, no matter what the current stimulus. The loop stays stuck until we find a way to break it.

When I decided to forget my pain and start going out, I broke the loop and my life changed. Proof came when I met a shy pixie at a porn reading who invited me home—and the address turned out to be the very same house of ill repute on Potrero Hill! I was strolling the musk-saturated, red-painted, dust bunny–hopping hallways of Generation Punk. At last.

Persistence. Persistence is one of my favorite character traits. I recommend trying it—it pays off big. I researched what felt like hundreds of healers until I found a physical therapist I loved. If she knocked on my door at 3:00 AM and asked for all my worldly possessions, I'd gladly hand them over, as long as she didn't also ask for what I still owe her.

Persistence with books and self-care has been as helpful as finding healers. I have a shelf of books, physiology treatises, about healing the back. If a book can teach me one new exercise to add to my morning back-care routine or help me understand one new scientific study that outlines the latest theory on the connection between mind, body, and pain, I figure it's priceless. I'll go to any length to refine my understanding of my back and get more in tune with the great wild goddess—or at least more in tune with my deep core muscles.

Taking risks. How does one persist and learn to break the cycle of pain? What worked for me was taking small steps, being lighthearted and gentle with my body, but continuing to cultivate new experiences.

Chronic pain made me unable to drive over a speed bump without conniptions. A million fears made my life a minefield: I couldn't sit long, laugh loud, carry groceries. To conquer these limitations, I learned to approach pain as the psychologists say to approach a phobia of snakes. First, one must merely *think* about a snake while breathing slowly. When people can do this successfully, they are then advised to approach a room with an actual snake in a cage while staying relaxed. And finally, they get to pet the snake. To live my life and not be afraid, I needed to learn how to approach each speed bump with a warm and forgiving breath. I reprogrammed myself so that when I was in the vicinity of any experience that had once caused me pain, I relaxed and imagined good things. It still helps.

The other trick was to risk *forgetting* about my back. I refrained from talking too much about my limitations. (I even read one study that found that inquiries from a spouse actually exacerbated chronic pain.) It was simply better not to focus on it. The result is that today, if my back gets bad, I continue with my exercises and my plans. If it's really wrenching, I take a day off, or maybe a little more. But soon I return to my normal life of NASCAR driving, snowboarding, and—even more challenging—hiking the steep hills of San Francisco.

Taking risks is what keeps my life worth living. I admit that most of my risks are now on the page in my new vocation as a novelist. But I will keep chancing something new, like a rip-roaring motorcycle ride on Christmas Eve—especially if it's with a brawny tattooed woman with a big smile. It's all good. I hope to dance, to play, to roll on the grass when I can. I remind myself to focus on the day, the sky, the hill, the person I'm with, and forget about the pain. When I can release the fear, I like to partake. And that's as much as I know. Dwelling in pain is overrated. I really do believe joy is how we make it through life.

Divorcing My Breasts

Liza Nelson

A s I type these words, I am wearing Levi's jeans without a belt, a long-sleeve stretchy black V-neck shirt, a wool scarf, striped socks, red sneakers, silver hoop earrings, white cotton underpants, and reading glasses. What I am not wearing is a bra.

I have not worn a bra for almost five years, not since the morning of my double mastectomy. Not even the pink, lace-trimmed Victoria's Secret bra I bought six weeks later; it rubbed my scars. I own a couple of stretchy cotton, pull-over-the-head onesies meant for twelve-year-olds, one in white and one in black, that I use under blouses that are too see-through. And I have a few of those camisoles that come with built-in shelves. I bought them because they looked so cute on my daughter, but I find them kind of constricting, so I don't use them much.

If you're reading this litany and thinking, *Poor woman,* don't.

I love feeling unbound, with no straps biting into my shoulders and no elastic squeezing my back. I love that no unwieldy chest is pulling the rest of me forward and down, as it did from age twelve to fifty-one. When I say I am glad I had a mastectomy with reconstructive surgery, I am not being sarcastic or ironic. I like—no, I love—my new, almost-flat chest.

I usually feel like a fake when the subject of my surgery comes up around other women. I dread the sympathetic murmur that implies courage on my part—or, worse, the nod of recognition that signifies having experienced similar adversity. I have no right to discuss the horror of breast cancer, the pain, the fear, and the deadliness that are all too real; like everyone my age, I've known too many victims. And I certainly don't qualify for sisterhood with cancer survivors. I was more of an evader. What for those other women was a dark cancer cloud was, for me, mostly a silver lining.

Not to say that I wasn't disturbed when I first suspected I might have something dangerously wrong. For years I was sent for extra tests to accompany my regularly scheduled mammogram, not, supposedly, because my breasts were oversize—although I suspect size did complicate the reading—but because their density made the tests hard to read, and because I tended to have benign cysts (again, nothing to do with size, supposedly). As usual, that September, the x-rays and sonograms showed nothing worrisome. Then, a month later, while undressing for bed, I noticed a few rust-colored specks clinging to the inside of my bra. That seemed a little odd. And the next night, there they were again in another bra, definitely bits of dried blood. I tested myself. When I squeezed, my right breast dripped a pale red discharge. Part of me knew that was not good, but only a small part.

"I know this is probably nothing," I apologized to my gynecologist's scheduling nurse after describing my symptom. I had the following month's calendar open, but she suggested I come in that afternoon. A few blood tests later, I was referred to a breast specialist who would see me the next day. It was four o'clock on a Friday afternoon when the nurse announced that the specialist was held up in an emergency, and that everyone in the full waiting room would have to reschedule. Everyone but one very sick-looking woman and me. Another member of the practice came over from the hospital just for us. After a brief examination, he set my lumpectomy/biopsy for the following Monday morning. I was nervous, but the procedure went smoothly. He didn't see anything to worry about and said I'd get the final results before our follow-up visit.

I assumed it was a good sign that no one from his office bothered to call me with those results before I showed up for my appointment ten days later. When the doctor walked into the examining room, I joked that no news was good news.

"Not exactly," he answered, after an awkward pause.

My memory of the rest of the conversation is a weird combination of crystal clear and very hazy. Bottom line: After a moment of a plunging certainty that I was dying, I found out I wasn't. I was in a gray zone, what my doctor called a precancerous condition. "Not a matter of if, but when," he repeated more than once. I could wait until the cancer blossomed and then be treated or make a preemptive strike with a mastectomy now. He didn't offer his preference. I'm not sure if I asked. I think I must have. I do know that I asked if I should do only the one breast, and he said no; once the cancer showed up, it would be systemic.

I felt very alone in that cubicle, unable to think straight about what the doctor's words really meant. You may be empathizing with my anxiety. But somewhere in the conversation, I mentioned that I'd been thinking about a breast reduction anyway, and he said a reduction was not an option. As he explained the procedure I could have—the double mastectomy, followed immediately by reconstructive surgery and using fat from my stomach to make new breasts— a silken thread of excitement began to wind its way inside my fears. I'd have small breasts and a flat tummy!

I'd been unhappily married to my breasts for as long as I could remember. Growing through the years from a B-cup to a C, to a DD and then to letters hovering around the Js, my breasts went from being an embarrassment to being an annoyance to being the bane of my existence. I did everything I could, short of cosmetic surgery, to conceal them. Now surgery was being handed to me as a matter of health.

In the weeks that followed, concerned friends put me in touch with their friends who had gone through mastectomies: Cancer Survivors. The more generously these women gave me their support and advice, the more I felt like an impostor. I was not one of them and I knew it. I explained I was precancerous, that the mastectomy would remove all risk of cancer, that unlike most of them I would not have to go through chemo and radiation. But their outpouring of empathy did not cease. They must have assumed that while I had avoided actual cancer, I was still sharing their struggle to overcome fear and womanly grief about giving up my breasts.

The fact that I was not struggling one bit was an embarrassing, certainly humbling admission I hesitated to make. I wanted to be part of their community, which felt morally elevated by the difficult choices they had to make, but I knew that my choice, unlike theirs, was a win/win no-brainer. Not only would I get a clean health slate, but I would also get the small boobs I'd always wanted and a flat stomach to boot.

Most of the women who talked to me were disturbed by having their feminine identity altered, but I was nonchalant, to say the least. I listened politely to suggestions that I get second opinions and research my condition on the Internet, but I knew all along what I was going to do. In fact, I was secretly relieved to have such a respectable excuse to do what I'd always wanted to do but could never quite justify. A friend of mine once admitted to having similar feelings when her husband finally left her, after years of a loveless marriage from which she had lacked the courage to escape. My breasts had finally given me an excuse to walk out on them without my appearing as superficial as I knew I probably was.

My primary concern during the next few weeks revolved around which doctor to use. I ruled out one because he looked at me as if I were crazy when I said I didn't want the silicone-enhanced C-cup he suggested.

*   *   *

Until the moment when the anesthesiologist counted me backward into unconsciousness, the potential risks of the surgery barely registered.

Despite the warnings that the recuperation period would be long and hard, I enjoyed it the same way I had relished the last days of each of my pregnancies. Yes, I was weak and in some pain for weeks, but I was also allowed to be totally self-absorbed, working on crossword puzzles in my recliner. And I suffered none of the genuine grief of most women whose breasts have been removed. Intellectually, I understood that losing a piece of oneself can cause deep trauma, and that because breasts represent both the maternal and the sexual aspects of a woman, the trauma of their loss may be all the greater. I went into my mastectomy expecting some trauma to surface afterward. It never did.

I was so anticipating life with my new boobs that, barely four weeks after surgery, I had my friend Trisha take me shopping. I needed (or, rather, wanted) a new dress to wear to a somewhat posh wedding that would be my B-cup debut. I was still sore and weak, barely able to walk from store to store, let alone lift my arms to get in and out of the dresses. After shopping for half an hour, I was wiped out, not sure I could make it back to Trisha's car. But I was also elated. I'd bought a strapless dress. Strapless. And a few weeks later I actually wore it. Me, in a strapless dress!

God, I loved having my new tight little tummy (with its Halloween-grimace scar), loved having firm (rock hard at first) little breasts that had no sag. Politically incorrect as it may sound, I still love them. And the change in my attitude, as well as in my body, has forced me to reconsider who I was as a woman before and after.

For all of my adolescent and adult life, I have been five-foot-three-and-a-half (a lot of pride going into that half), frizzy haired, with undeniably Semitic features and complexion. I still am that person. For years I wanted to be straight haired and straight nosed. I still am not. But most of all, as I aged and my breasts grew (and sagged), I wanted to be flat chested.

*   *   *

The boobs sprouted in sixth grade. Susie Tippett and I were the first ones to need—and I mean need—bras. But she also had straight hair and a face that was delicately perfect. In retrospect, my curves probably intimidated, rather than grossed out, the boys, but I had no awareness. After a kid in my science class made a snide remark that I was showing off when I sat up straight, I went into permanent slump mode. Throughout high school, my identity was bound up in being smart and plain, the girl boys befriended instead of boyfriended.

There was some talk of breast reduction before I left for college, but I balked—fortunately, as it happens, because a breast reduction might have increased my chances of undetected cancer. I balked only because my mother made the suggestion. Since well before my teens, whatever Mom wanted for me, I didn't want. Her pleasure in buying me clothes was matched only by my discomfort in trying them on. I hemmed up old skirts with safety pins rather than buying new ones. I eschewed makeup and stopped the expensive professional hair straightening that left burn scars on my scalp. I would never admit that looks mattered as much to me as they did to her. Or maybe I thought how I looked was hopeless. I couldn't look the part she wanted—a large woman herself, my mother judges beauty according to thinness—so why bother to try? In the era of Twiggy, my unfashionable breasts became the symbol of my every failure.

I scrambled happily aboard the life raft of feminism when it burst upon the zeitgeist midway through college. What a relief to let my hair go natural and turn my self-consciousness into a matter of conscience! I could self-righteously hide my body inside baggy work shirts and jeans. In all the consciousness-raising groups I joined, I don't remember ever discussing my discomfort with my body. And, despite all the lip service I paid to sexual freedom, I allowed no one, man nor woman, to see me naked.

Basically, I felt like a slug. Even after I met and married my husband, I found it hard to believe any man could consider my body attractive. I picked my wedding dress for its high collar and long sleeves. The important criterion in my clothed life—in all aspects of my life—was based on what made me (meaning my chest) look small. I traded in my college work shirts for loose tops that hung below my waist. I wore a lot of black. I loved winter because bulky sweaters were forgiving. I hated summer because it required light fabrics and short sleeves. I never wore a sleeveless top or anything that tucked in. Bathing suits? Forget it. My only happy bathing-suit experience occurred when I was pregnant. I had a wonderful Pepto-Bismol–pink suit with a big bow. Its flattering balloon shape slimmed my thighs while disguising both stomach and breasts. Actually, many of my happiest clothing memories revolve around pregnancy—that cute black velvet, the huge red corduroy—when being top heavy was temporarily acceptable.

Unfortunately, when I wasn't pregnant, I still felt as if I were all boob, waist to neck. After my first child was born, I got down to twenty-seven-inch-waist jeans. I had to have been thin, but even now, when I look at a photo from that period of my life, all I see is how matronly I appeared. No matter what I wore, I felt lumpy and dumpy, trapped and uncomfortable. It shouldn't have mattered so much, yet it did.

Shopping for clothes was bearable. Shopping for bras was humiliating. Other young women wore bras with patterns and flowers and maybe lace; I wore big cotton things held together by what felt like iron boning. Normal bras did not fit. When minimizers came on the market, they didn't fit either. I squeezed myself into my old-fashioned brassieres, ignoring the bunching of breast above the cup's rim as the day went on—another reason to keep those blouses loose. Eventually, I discovered a brand called Edith Lance, which squashed flailing, blubbery flesh against my chest and cost three times as much as a minimizing bra. It did not give me what anyone would call a youthful look, but I no longer felt like an ocean liner every time I crossed a room.

My breasts took over my sense of self. I was never unaware of them, and everything I did physically, I did in terms of them: from walking into a room (slumped), to driving the car (seatbelts were impossible), to sleeping (flattening one side or the other into a bat wing). I didn't know there was another way to feel about myself besides imprisoned, so I almost stopped noticing my own discomfort. That discomfort's postmastectomy disappearance, like an ache that has suddenly gone, has heightened my awareness of how strong it was.

How I choose to dress has been the obvious symbol of the change in me since the mastectomy. Shortly after my surgery, my sister sent me five ribbed tank tops from Old Navy, each in a different color. They scared me when I took them out of the box. Five years later, I still wear them almost every day during the summer. Faded and stained, they make me feel good. However, that strapless dress I bought for the wedding has not seen the light of day again. Nor have a lot of the clothes I bought around that time; these overly dressy or trendy or youthful confections have ended up sitting in my closet until I give them to Goodwill. It took a while to grope my way to a clothing comfort zone—I had to experiment to find what fit emotionally as well as physically.

I love how I dress now: in jeans, T-shirts, and turtlenecks with shawls, the occasional skirt with tights. I actually tuck tops in and have been known to cinch a belt, although my waist may actually be wider since the surgery. I suppose I dress the way I wanted to dress at age eighteen. Whatever I wear, I like to think I'm letting my personality come through more than I used to.

On a deeper level, I have no doubt that my physical change has altered my personality, and maybe even my character. For a long time, my lack of physical confidence permeated my intellectual confidence. On the one hand, I relied on being the smart one instead of the pretty one; on the other hand, I hated being the smart one. Eventually, I stopped being either. I don't want to make myself out as a misfit: I had friends; I had boyfriends and then a husband and kids. I worked in journalism and theater. But I was way beyond normal insecurity, always. I was a moody nightmare, self-doubting and self-loathing. Ask my shrink, or my husband. To blame the size of my breasts seems ludicrous, but I often did.

The year before my cancer scare, I published my first novel. I was thrilled. It was, excepting my children, the great creative accomplishment of my life. And yet . . . I did not quite allow myself to bask in the glory of being published. Instead, my joy burned like a small night-light in a corner of my soul. I did not push the book, or myself as a novelist, into the world. I preferred invisibility.

Then I had my mastectomy. Certainly, the scare of facing mortality had its effect: I was ready to grasp life more firmly. But what felt different was less facing the possibility of death than my sudden comfort with myself as a living woman. I became braver. I spoke more honestly to myself about what really mattered, what I really wanted from life.

After years spent tamping down the girl in me, I have let the life-affirming fun lover float free. Although that old bad habit of unnecessary self-deprecation lingers, I have stopped being afraid of seeming or being quirky, stopped trying to disappear into the woodwork. Not that I'm suddenly more ambitious in conventional ways. If anything, I've let some of those old pressures to prove myself evaporate. I am not only physically, but also emotionally and mentally, lighter. I have been working away on my second novel, allowing myself to love the process without worrying whether it will get published. I am learning Spanish and I am blowing glass. I am making new friends after years of semi-isolation.

Was I a different person with elephant-ear breasts than I am now with squished, flat, crabappleish ones? Who would I have been at thirty with trim breasts and a body that didn't shame me? Would I have been less socially awkward, less afraid to take career risks, less tense? Obviously, lots of big-breasted women do not suffer the same insecurities I did (although I wonder what a study might show). Was I the kind of person who needed to use a physical imperfection as my scapegoat? If so, why don't I need one now when I am fifty-six, with wrinkles and sags, but feel remarkably girlish? Did changing my body make that much of a difference? Maybe, although I don't think I could justify cosmetic surgery to myself even now. Although I'd look younger, and the idea of the knife doesn't scare me, I'm afraid that if I started, I couldn't stop at one procedure. It's the same rationale that bans Oreos from my kitchen cupboard.

After the surgery, my wisewoman friend Paula, to whom I had confided my honest reactions all along, remarked that I had simply become myself, had finally embraced the small-breasted person inside me. The weight I carried on my chest all those years was both the excuse I hid behind and the reason I genuinely felt off-kilter, inside and out. After all, my arms are still flabby, my hair still frizzy. My hips stretch wider than ever. My stomach might be a bit flatter than it was during my presurgical eating binge, but I am not what anyone would call svelte. I still have the same birthmarks on the old skin that covers my new breasts, along with new scars under my armpits and across my stomach. I could not care less. My body is not perfect, but it suits me now. I feel, though it amazes me to write this, comfortable with myself. What more could I ask?

Acknowledgments

This anthology is so much more than a collection of essays; it is an assemblage of emotions, confidences, and experiences entrusted to me by twenty-six talented authors and exceptional women. The generosity of spirit, the support and the encouragement offered by each woman in this book have made this project a moving and delightful experience. Therefore, first and foremost and above all else, I thank the authors.

To Anne Connolly, Brooke Warner, Andie East, and the team at Seal Press, my thanks for your support during this project, and for giving your blessings to the diverse and sometimes unexpected story each author wished to tell.

A special thank-you to Laura Mazer for shepherding through this process with humor and a keen eye.

Heartfelt thanks to Jill Marsal, from the Sandra Dijkstra Literary Agency, for sharing this wonderful ride with me, guiding me along the right road, and believing in my ability to arrive safely at our destination. And thanks to the Farley's crowd—Ralph Anary, Ruth Price, and Mary Wasserman.

My loving thanks to my family: Alisa and Eugene Law, Sophia and Olivia; Matthew Sosnick; Elizabeth Zackheim; Michele Zackheim and Charles Ramsburg. You are always by my side, in heart and spirit. Your love provides so much of the energy that drives this imperfect machine.

About the Contributors

BARBARA ABERCROMBIE has published three novels and numerous children's books, including the prize-winning *Charlie Anderson*. Her latest books are *Writing Out the Storm* (St. Martin's Press) and *Courage and Craft: Writing Your Life into Story* (New World Library). Her essays and articles have appeared in many publications, including the *Los Angeles Times, The Baltimore Sun,* and *The Christian Science Monitor*. She teaches creative writing at UCLA Extension and conducts writing workshops for the Wellness Community. www.writingtime.net

REGINA ANAVY has a degree in French from UC Berkeley. She has been a political organizer, legal assistant, editor, environmental researcher, and, more recently, a translator of Cuban literature. She has written a number of magazine articles, has been published in the *San Francisco Chronicle,* and is the editor of *Larry's Letters,* a compilation of family correspondence recalling the life of a Jewish family in North Dakota, and a soldier's experiences in World War II. She lives in San Francisco when she is not traveling.

SUSANNE DUNLAP, author of the historical novels *Emilie's Voice* and *Liszt's Kiss* (Simon & Schuster) is a classically trained pianist who spent fifteen years of her adult life writing advertising copy before returning to school for her PhD in music history from Yale. A Bread Loaf attendee in the summer of 2003, she writes historical fiction that draws on her musical background. www.emiliesvoice.com

MARGOT BETH DUXLER is a licensed clinical psychologist in private practice in San Francisco. She is the author of the psychobiography *Seduction: A Portrait of Anaïs Nin* (Edgework Books). Her fiction has appeared in a number of literary journals. With W. A. Smith, she served as coeditor of fiction for the *Five Fingers Review*; with Edouard Muller, she worked as co-translator for the first edition of Gault-Millau's *The Best of Paris*. She is a professional fiddler and has performed and recorded with Golden Bough and the Celtic Wonder Band. She is working on a novel and a collection of short stories.

LOUISA ERMELINO is the author of three novels: *Joey Dee Gets Wise, The Black Madonna,* and *The Sisters Mallone.* She has worked at *Time* magazine, *People,* and *InStyle,* has published short stories, reviews, and articles, and is the reviews director at *Publishers Weekly* magazine. www.louisaermelino.com

ABBY FRUCHT is the author of a collection of stories, *Fruit of the Month,* and the novels *Snap, Licorice, Are You Mine?; Life Before Death; and Polly's Ghost.* In addition to the Iowa Prize for Short Fiction, she has been awarded two National Endowment for the Arts Fellowships and a Quality Paperback Book Club New Voices Award. She has reviewed books and written personal essays for numerous magazines and newspapers nationwide, lives with her family in Wisconsin, and teaches at the Vermont College MFA in Writing program. www.abbyfrucht.net

DEBORAH GRABIEN is the author of *Eyes in the Fire; Plainsong; Fire Queen; And Then Put Out the Light; The Weaver and the Factory Maid* (named by the *Library Journal* as one of the five best mysteries of 2003); *The Famous Flower of Serving Men;* and *Matty Groves.* Future work includes *The Fourth Ring* (anthology, 2006) and *The New-Slain Knight* (St. Martins Minotaur, 2007). www.deborahgrabien.com

MASHA HAMILTON is the author of three novels. *The Distance Between Us* was named one of the best books of 2004 by the *Library Journal,* and *Staircase of a Thousand Steps* was named a BookSense choice and Barnes & Noble Discover Great New Writers selection. Her third novel, *The Camel Bookmobile,* a BookSense pick, is about a camel-powered library in Africa and the American librarian who helps organize it. Hamilton has reported from Afghanistan, the Middle East, and Moscow for the *Los Angeles Times,* The Associated Press, and others. www.mashahamilton.com

SUSAN ITO edited *A Ghost at Heart's Edge: Stories and Poems of Adoption* and has had her stories and essays published in *Hip Mama, Growing Up Asian American, Making More Waves,* the

Bellevue Literary Review, The Asian Pacific American Journal, the *Santa Barbara Review,* and more. She has received residencies and fellowships at MacDowell Colony, Hedgebrook, and Blue Mountain Center. One of her short stories was nominated for a Pushcart Prize. www.readingwritingliving.wordpress.com

CARRIE KABAK is the author of *Cover the Butter,* a 2005 BookSense bestseller. She has received commendation as an illustrator from *Writer's Digest* and was named illustrator of the month by the Society of Children's Writers and Artists. Her second novel, *Tarts and Sinners,* is in progress. www.carriekabak.com

CAROLINE LEAVITT has written eight novels, including *Coming Back to Me* and the BookSense Notable *Girls in Trouble.* Awarded a New York Foundation of the Arts Grant in Fiction and nominated for a National Magazine Award in Personal Essay, she was a finalist for a Nickelodeon Screenwriting Fellowship and was a second-prize winner of the Goldenberg Literary Prize. Her work has appeared in such publications as *Salon, Redbook,* the *Chicago Tribune, The Washington Post,* and *People.* She lives with her husband, writer Jeff Tamarkin, and their young son, Max, in Hoboken, New Jersey. www.carolineleavitt.com

AIMEE LIU is the author of *Gaining: The Truth About Life After Eating Disorders.* She has also written three novels, *Flash House, Cloud Mountain, Face,* and a memoir, *Solitaire,* and has coauthored numerous books on psychological and medical topics.

Her work has appeared in a variety of literary journals and magazines and in the anthologies *My California; Meeting Across the River; Grandmother Histories;* and *I'm on My Way Running.* Liu earned her MFA from Bennington College and now teaches creative writing in Goddard College's Port Townsend MFA program. www.aimeeliu.net

KATE MALOY is the author of the memoir *A Stone Bridge North: Reflections in a New Life* (Counterpoint, 2002) and coauthor (with Maggie Jones Patterson) of *Birth or Abortion? Private Struggles in a Political World* (Plenum, 1992; Perseus, 2001). Her work has been published in national magazines, online at VerbSap.com and Literarymama.com, and in *The Readerville Journal* and *Choice* (MacAdam/Cage). Kate is the recipient of a Vermont Council for the Arts grant. Her first novel will soon be released by Algonquin Books. She now lives with her husband on the central coast of Oregon. www.katemaloy.com

ELLIE MCGRATH is the author of *My One and Only: The Special Experience of the Only Child* (William Morrow). She has been a staff writer and editor for *Time* magazine, an editor at *Women's Sports and Fitness* and *Self* magazines, and a journalist-in-residence. www.mcwittypress.com

LIZA NELSON is the author of the novels *Playing Botticelli* and *The Book of Feasts,* which was nominated for a James Beard Award. She has published poems in various journals and has worked as a freelance journalist, a dramaturge, a part-time teacher, and a bookkeeper. She lives in rural Georgia.

SARA NELSON is the author of *So Many Books, So Little Time.* She is a contributor to *Glamour, The New York Times, The Wall Street Journal,* the *Chicago Tribune, The New York Observer,* and the *New York Post,* and is editor in chief of *Publishers Weekly.*

KATIA NOYES has worked as a roofer, math tutor, journalist, go-go dancer, and content developer. Her debut novel, *Crashing America,* was a BookSense Notable Book, selected as one of the ten best gay/lesbian books of 2005 by Amazon.com and the United Kingdom's Rainbow Network, and nominated for the Northern California Book Award, the Publishing Triangle Award, and the Lambda Literary Award. Her short stories have been published by Cleis and Down There Press. She lives in San Francisco. www.katianoyes.com

CHRISTINE KEHL O'HAGAN is the author of *Benediction at the Savoia* and the memoir *The Book of Kehls,* both of which received starred Kirkus reviews; the latter was selected by *Kirkus Reviews* as one of the best books of 2005. Her essays have appeared in *Between Friends; The Day My Father Died; Lives Through Literature; Facts on File: The American Novel; The New York Times;* and *Newsday.* A recipient of the Jerry Lewis Writing Awards, O'Hagan is working on a new novel, *Arabella's Waltz.* www.christinekehlohagan.com

JOAN PRICE is the author of *Better Than I Ever Expected: Straight Talk About Sex After Sixty* (Seal Press, 2006), *The Anytime, Anywhere Exercise Book,* and several others. She's an advocate for ageless sexuality and a fitness instructor, a line-dance teacher, author, and nationally recognized motivational speaker who draws upon her own recoveries from near-fatal accidents to convey the importance of exercise, healthy living, and keeping joy in our lives. www.joanprice.com

ELIZABETH ROSNER is a poet, essayist, and author of two best-selling novels. *The Speed of Light* received the Harold U. Ribalow Prize and the Great Lakes Colleges New Writer's Award for Fiction. In France, and published as *Des demons sur les épaules,* the novel was a finalist for the prestigious Prix Femina and was awarded the Prix France Bleu Gironde. Translated into nine languages, it was twice a BookSense 76 selection and one of Borders' Original Voices. Ms. Rosner's second novel, *Blue Nude,* was published in 2006. Her poetry chapbook, *Gravity,* was one of the Select Poets Series published by Small Poetry Press and is in its fourteenth printing. Her recent essays have appeared in *The New York Times Magazine, Elle,* and other national publications. www.elizabethrosner.com

ROCHELLE JEWEL SHAPIRO is a well-known psychic and author of the autobiographical novel *Miriam the Medium,* which was nominated for the Harold U. Ribelow Award and will be published in Holland. Shapiro has published articles in *Newsweek, My Turn,* and *The New York Times.* Articles about her have appeared in *Redbook* and the "Long Island" section of *The New York Times.* As a psychic, she is an international radio celebrity and has a large private practice of the famous, the infamous, and the average Joe. She teaches "Writing the

Personal Essay" for UCLA online and reviews for *Kirkus*.
www.miriamthemedium.com

CLEA SIMON is the author of *Mad House: Growing Up in the Shadows of Mentally Ill Siblings; Fatherless Women: How We Change After We Lose Our Dads;* and *The Feline Mystique: On the Mysterious Connection Between Women and Cats.* She is also the author of the Theda Krakow mysteries *Mew Is for Murder* and *Cattery Row.* Simon is a regular contributor to *The Boston Globe, The Boston Phoenix,* and the *San Francisco Chronicle.* www.cleasimon.com

LEORA SKOLKIN-SMITH is a cofounder of the Emmett Till/Anne Frank Program, a multicultural educational initiative for African-American and Jewish youth in Brooklyn. Her first novel, *Edges,* was published by Glad Day Books and was awarded a stipend from the Pen/Faulkner Foundation National Schools Program. It was also a *Bloomsbury Review* favorite pick of the last twenty-five years, a Jewish Book Council selection, and a selection of both the National Women's Studies Association and the Miami International Book Festival. Her second novel is in progress. www.leoraskolkinsmith.com

ELLEN SUSSMAN is the author of the novel *On a Night Like This,* which became a *San Francisco Chronicle* bestseller and has been translated into six languages. Her anthology, *Bad Girls: 25 Writers Misbehave,* a collection of literary essays by women writers, was published in July 2007. She has published a dozen short stories in literary and commercial magazines and has been awarded fellowships from Writers at Work, Wesleyan Writers Conference, and Virginia Center for the Creative Arts. www.ellensussman.com

SALLY TERRELL is an associate professor of English at Tunxis Community College, where she teaches writing. She chaired CCET, an organization of English professors in Connecticut. She was chapter editor for "The American City: Dreams and Nightmares" in *Reading Our Histories, Understanding Our Cultures* (Longman), has contributed creative nonfiction and poetry to the literary journal *Otto*, and is at work on a memoir.

HANNAH YAKIN is the author of adult and children's fiction, including *Here Is Your Bridegroom; What's in a Shell?; The Gottlieb Menagerie* (broadcast by the BBC and translated into French, Spanish, and Russian); *Angela, The Land of Milk and Honey* (broadcast by the BBC); *Mimicry; Aristotle and Autostrada; and Spectacles.* Yakin's short stories and articles (in Dutch, English, and Hebrew) have appeared in literary magazines, as well as in *The Jerusalem Post* and *Waves.* Her story "Of Tortoises and Other Jews" became *Yan's Daughter,* a play by Patricia O'Donovan, regularly produced in Israel since 2004. Born in Holland, the author lives in Jerusalem.

About the Editor

© Melissa Dodd

Victoria Zackheim is the author of *The Bone Weaver*, a novel, and editor of *The Other Woman* (Warner 2007). She teaches creative writing in the UCLA Writers' Program and is a frequent guest speaker for women's organizations. She is the writer and story producer of the documentary film *Suffer the Little Children: Frances Kelsey and the Story of Thalidomide* (Rosemarie Reed Productions/Films for Thought). www.victoriazackheim.com.